# Life Through God's Word

# Life Through God's Word

### PSALM 119

Christopher J. H. Wright

**Keswick**
ministries
bringing the Word alive

**Authentic**

LONDON ● COLORADO SPRINGS ● HYDERABAD

Reprinted 2007
13  12  11  10  09  08  07    8  7  6  5  4  3  2

First published in 2006 by Keswick Ministries and Authentic Media
9 Holdom Avenue, Bletchley, Milton Keynes, Bucks., MK1 1QR
1820 Jet Stream Drive, Colorado Springs, CO  80921, USA
OM Authentic Media, Medchal Road, Jeedimetla Village,
Secunderabad 500 055, A.P., India
www.authenticmedia.co.uk
Authentic Media is a division of IBS-STL UK., a company limited by guarantee
(registered charity no. 270162)

**British Library Cataloguing in Publication Data**
A catalogue record for this book is available from the British Library

ISBN-13: 978-1-85078-694-8
ISBN-10: 1-85078-694-1

Cover design by Sam Redwood
Print Management by Adare Carwin
Printed in Great Britain by J.H. Haynes & Co., Sparkford

To
The Chad Branch
SIL

# Contents

The aim of this study guide      ix
Preface      xi
Introduction      xiii

■ SECTION 1   PERSONAL COMMITMENT AND THE WORD OF TRUTH      1

Chapter 1   God's word as the focus of faith and commitment      6

Chapter 2   God's word as the focus of love and obedience      14

■ SECTION 2   PERSONAL GUIDANCE AND THE WORD OF LIGHT      25

Chapter 3   Light for the path      29

Chapter 4   Learning for the pupil      41

■ SECTION 3   PERSONAL SIN AND THE WORD OF GRACE      51

Chapter 5   Awareness of sin      55

Chapter 6   Answering sin – through our minds and wills      62

Chapter 7   Answering sin – through our emotions and faith      70

■ SECTION 4   PERSONAL STRUGGLE AND THE WORD OF LAMENT      77

Chapter 8   When life gets tough      81

Chapter 9   How does it feel?      88

Chapter 10   Pressing on      96

■ SECTION 5   PERSONAL RENEWAL AND THE WORD OF LIFE      105

Chapter 11   Threats to life      110

Chapter 12   Sources of life      119

Conclusion      137

## THE AIM OF THIS STUDY GUIDE

The aim of this study guide is to help bridge the gap between the Bible world and our own. Chris Wright's exposition of Psalm 119 has vibrant meaning for us as believers in the 21st Century. The questions that follow help relate the principles he draws out to our own lives and situations. You can use this guide either for your own devotional time with God or as part of a group. Enjoy your study!

## USING THIS BOOK FOR PERSONAL STUDY

Begin by praying and reading through the passage and commentary a number of times before looking at the questions. You may find it helpful to note down your answers to the questions and any other thoughts you may have. Putting pen to paper will help you think through the issues and how they specifically apply to your own situation. It will also be encouraging to look back over all that God has been teaching you!

Talk about what you're learning with a friend. Pray together that you'll be able to apply all these new lessons to your life.

## USING THIS BOOK IN SMALL GROUPS

In preparation for the study, pray and then read the passage of Scripture and commentary over a number of times. Use other resource material such as a Bible dictionary or atlas if they would be helpful. Each week think through what materials you need for the study – a flip chart, pens and paper, other Bible translations, worship tapes?

At the top of each chapter we have stated the aim – this is the heart of the passage and the truth you want your group to take away with them. With this in mind, decide which questions and activities you should spend most time on. Add questions that would be helpful to your group or particular church situation.

Before people come, encourage them to read the passage and commentary that you will be studying that week.

Make sure you leave time at the end of the study for people to 'Reflect and Respond' so they are able to apply what they are learning to their own life situation.

# Preface

It was a surprise and a privilege when Jonathan Lamb, then Chair of the Keswick Council, invited me to give morning Bible Readings at Keswick in July 1998. I accepted gladly. My enthusiasm dimmed somewhat when Jonathan later wrote to say that the Council wondered if I would like to consider a series of five expositions of Psalm 119. That was more of a challenge, and it was some time before I agreed that it was a challenge well worth tackling.

The first tactical decision I made was that I did not think I could handle the longest psalm in the book simply through verse-by-verse exposition over five days. So I read it and re-read it, at home, on train journeys, all over the place, until eventually several key themes began to crystallize in my mind. These then took shape as the five Bible expositions that bore the titles of the five main sections of this book. I hoped this was an acceptable way of handling this wonderful but dauntingly large poem.

Recently, I heard from a good friend who is a preaching elder in a large church in the USA. He had taken Psalm 119 with a group of about 20 men for their weekly study. He asked each one to memorize one of the 22 sections of eight verses and then to produce their own piece of poetry that expressed for themselves something of their own life's faith and struggles comparable to the Psalmist. He suggested that they could then recite both before the group as a prelude to discussion and prayer around that section of the psalm. Well that sounded wonderful, but we didn't have 22 weeks at Keswick, and several thousand personal poems would have been difficult to handle. Readers might like to try the idea for themselves, though.

Anyway, I did what I did, and I am glad now to have the opportunity to put the material into this format for personal or group Bible study. I am thankful to Jonathan Lamb for the original invitation and to Keswick Ministries and Authentic for seeing it through to publication and to Lucy Atherton for her editing expertise.

I worked on the writing up of the final section, Personal Renewal and the Word of Life, while spending a week in the company of a fine group of people – the fifty or so members of the Chad Branch of SIL. I was their Bible speaker for a week's retreat at their annual conference. For me it was a time also of great encouragement and blessing, in listening to them talk about their Bible translation work into many of the 125 different languages of that country that did not yet have the Bible in written form. Theirs is a commitment to the truth, relevance and life-giving power of God's word that reminded me again and again of the sentiments of Psalm 119. And theirs too are some of the struggles, stresses and suffering that the writer of this psalm clearly endured. So this book is dedicated to them, with admiration for their labours, praise to God for what he is accomplishing through them and gratitude for a week of blessing spent in their company.

*Chris Wright*
*February 2006*

# Introduction

The story is told of how William Grimshaw, a Puritan minister in Haworth, Yorkshire, in the 1740s, would set his congregation reciting a psalm while he went out to chase reluctant parishioners into church. If there were too many absentees from church in the nearby pub, he would set the church reciting Psalm 119 to give himself time to do so.

Everybody knows that Psalm 119 is the longest psalm in the book. And anybody who has ever read it even rapidly can see that it refers in almost every single verse to God's word or God's law. For that reason some people find it repetitive and tedious, and don't dig deeper which is a pity, for in fact Psalm 119 is a superbly crafted poetic achievement.

Some of the psalms are called acrostics. That is, they are alphabetical. Each line of these psalms begins with successive letters of the Hebrew alphabet, which has 22 letters. Psalms 111 and 112 are good examples, and they match each other thematically as well, since Psalm 111 is about the righteousness of God, while Psalm 112 is about the righteousness of the person who fears God. But the author of Psalm 119 was not content with a single line per letter. To do justice to the great outpouring of his heart, this poet needed eight lines per letter, so he composed a vast tapestry of a psalm, with 22 stanzas of eight lines each, starting with a new letter of the alphabet each time. In many English Bibles we can see that Hebrew letter or at least its name, at the heading of each next block of eight verses.

Then, to enrich his work, the poet found eight different ways of talking about the word of God. Some of them are similar, but they do have subtle shades of meaning. Here they are in the order they are introduced to us in the psalm. The translation given in italics is the one normally used in the NIV.

| Verse | Hebrew word | Approximate meaning |
|-------|-------------|---------------------|
| 1 | *Torah* | *The law* as a whole; basically meaning guidance |
| 2 | *'edoth* | *Statutes*, testimonies, witness |
| 4 | *Piqqudim* | *Precepts*, detailed instructions |
| 5 | *Huqqim* | *Decrees*, inscribed and binding |
| 6 | *Miswoth* | *Commands*, orders |
| 7 | *Mispatim* | *Laws*, judgments, decisions, precedents |
| 9 | *Dabar* | *Word* |
| 38 | *'imrah* | *Promise* |

So these words are all woven together, like the threads of a tapestry, giving texture and colour. Or to change the metaphor, they provide the constant background rhythm of the poem while the themes change and the moods ebb and flow.

The paradox is, however, that although these words pervade the psalm, it would be wrong to say that this is simply a 'Psalm in honour of the Law' – as a kind of dry and dusty commendation to encourage subservience or, even worse, legalism. In fact, the psalm is not really about the law directly at all. Apart from the first three verses, the whole poem is *entirely addressed to God*. The most repeated words in the psalm are not words for the law, but 'you' and 'your'. That is, this psalm is highly relational. This is an extended prayer, a testimony, a plea, a complaint, a reassurance, that comes out of deep personal experience and profound emotional and intimate relationship with God. That's what we should discover as we study it carefully together.

So what benefit will there be for us in soaking ourselves in Psalm 119 for however long it takes to work through this book? I think we will find that it mirrors for us what is probably the common experience of so many believers. Here is someone who not only speaks to us, but speaks for us. What kind of person can we see behind this poetic work of art? I believe we see

- *A person with a strong love for God and for God's word.*
- *A person with a deep desire to live in a way that pleases God.*
- *A person who knows that this will bring joy, blessing, freedom and fullness of life.*
- *A person who wants to walk in the right way and avoid doing what is wrong and sinful, but needs help to do so.*
- *A person who is going through experiences of real stress, difficulty, external threat and internal fear, exhaustion, failure and vulnerability, and shows signs of depression.*
- *A person who longs for God to meet those needs and to renew, protect and sustain their life.*
- *A person who knows the character of God to be loving, gracious, righteous and merciful – and knows all this from the Scriptures.*

If some or all of those things find an echo in your heart, then here is a good travelling companion for your journey.

Rather than try to work through the psalm verse by verse, it seemed better to identify some of the major themes that recur again and again and to look at those in depth. Each section begins with a recommended portion of the psalm to read that focuses on the theme we will be about to study in the chapters in that section of the book. Those studying the psalm as part of a group may find it helpful to read these verses aloud. Here in advance are the topics we shall consider. Each one is a pair – putting together the subjective feeling, need or intention of the Psalmist and the objective dimension of God's word that spoke to his personal reality.

| Section | Topic | Recommended portion (verses) |
|---------|-------|------------------------------|
| 1 | Personal Commitment and the Word of Truth | 57-64 |
| 2 | Personal Guidance and the Word of Light | 97-104, 105 |
| 3 | Personal Sin and the Word of Grace | 9-16 |
| 4 | Personal Struggle and the Word of Lament | 81-88 |
| 5 | Personal Renewal and the Word of Life | 153-160 |

But before we start on the study, I suggest that we find time to read through the whole psalm, slowly and appreciatively, trying to savour its moods and passions, and to pray the Psalmist's prayer with him.

# Personal Commitment and the Word of Truth

**Recommended reading: Psalm 119:57-64**

# Personal Commitment and the Word of Truth

## INTRODUCTION TO SECTION 1

I have been involved for many years in the world of cross-cultural mission, partly through working in India for five years, but much more through the 13 years that I worked at All Nations Christian College, before joining the Langham Partnership. Both at All Nations, and in visiting many of its former students since in their places of service, I have been continually amazed at and humbled by the depth of commitment shown by men and women in mission. And what I observe most clearly is that such depth of commitment flows from core beliefs. What these folk are committed to doing is something that bubbles up irrepressibly from a sense of ultimate values, from that well of deep and even subconscious convictions that form a person's worldview.

● *I have marvelled at medical and paramedical folk exposing themselves to the horrors and dangers of Afghanistan in its worst times because they are convinced that every human being – of whatever faith, with all their limbs or none – matters personally to God and is to be loved and served for his sake. One former student returned from there and spoke at college. At the end he casually took some spent bullets from his pocket and said he would give them to anybody wanting to pray for him. He had dug them out of the walls of his bedroom, his lampshade and his door, while living in the war zone.*

- *I read the words of a midwife in the deserts of North Africa, struggling with her own appalling back pain, talking of the infinite worth of every tiny baby she delivers, and the deep grief she shares with any mother at losing a child of God.*

- *I have seen Christian conservationists handling tiny birds with tender affection, not out of sentimentality, but out of the conviction that all creation has value, and if not a sparrow falls to earth without our heavenly Father, then it is worthy of our care too.*

- *I have written part of this book while sharing in a retreat with Bible translators in Chad, and listened to one lady's struggle with chronic exhaustion syndrome and other debilitating illness, but battling on with the translation of portions of Scripture into a tribal language. 'It is the word of God, after all,' she smiles. 'They need it. God gave me the skills to give it to them. What else can I do?'*

Such stories could be multiplied. They are stories of deep commitment, but in all cases that commitment flows out of ultimate core beliefs.

One thing that is obvious about the person who wrote Psalm 119 is that he is totally *committed* – heart and soul, body, mind and spirit – to God, to God's word and to God's ways. And the reason for this passionate commitment is also not hard to detect. It is because the Psalmist's whole *worldview* is shaped by the fundamental conviction that God's word is true and trustworthy, so much so that he can build his whole life upon it – even when it is a tough and uncomfortable life he is building. His *commitment to* God's word is founded on his *convictions about* God's word.

So let us look, then, at some of the ways this Psalmist articulated his convictions about God's word – by which he is most often referring to God's law. We find that God's word is the focus of his belief and trust, the focus of his love and delight and the focus of his obedient commitment. Here is someone who is responding to God's word intellectually, emotionally and behaviourally. Head, heart and hands – all three are engaged.

CHAPTER 1

# God's word as the focus of faith and commitment

---

*Aim: To focus on the transcendent qualities of God's word*

---

**FOCUS ON THE THEME**
What are the things you care most about in life? Morals, justice, equality, evangelism? In what ways does the Bible shape your core beliefs and commitments?

A key statement to start us off is the simple affirmation of verse 66: 'I believe in your commands.'

The word 'believe' here means to have complete confidence. The Psalmist is saying, 'I put all my intellectual trust and faith in your commands.' This is far more than blind obedience or legalistic adherence to a code of rules. What he means is, 'I understand these words, I agree with them, I am committed to their truth and validity, I lean on them, I know I can depend on them.' He repeats this conviction in verse 86. He is not interested merely in obeying rules – he is exercising intelligent faith in the trustworthiness of the commands of God: 'All your commands are trustworthy.'

Why is this? What reasons does the Psalmist give for such intellectual and moral confidence in God's word? There is a whole chain of verses threaded through the psalm that support this confidence with strong affirmations about God's word. They may be grouped into three categories. The Psalmist asserts and celebrates about the word of God that it is *eternal*, that it is morally *righteous* and that it is *true*. Let's look at each of these.

## ITS ETERNAL NATURE OR UNIVERSALITY

It is, after all, the word of God, so it inevitably shares God's eternal, transcendent nature. If there is only one, true, living God who owns, rules and fills the whole universe, then the word of that God must likewise be universal. And this is what the Psalmist affirms. Read the following three sections and consider their vast implications.

Your word, O LORD, is eternal;
   it stands firm in the heavens.Your faithfulness continues
through all generations;
   you established the earth and it endures (vv89-91).

● *How does verse 91 set God's law in a universal framework?*


To all perfection I see a limit;
   but your commands are boundless (v96).

● *Even the best that humans can achieve is limited. By contrast, what does this verse say about God's commands?*
● *What does 'boundless' mean?*
● *Think about the difference between the local context in which the commands were given, and the perennial relevance they have in all times and places. How do we respond to God's commands today?*

Long ago I learned from your statutes
    that you established them to last for ever (v152).

● *Why do you think God gave his law? What was his
intention?*

We should not think that these verses mean God's laws
were somehow timeless in the sense of being abstract
principles unrelated to any particular local context. On the
contrary, all God's words were given within a specific
history and culture, and that is why they had such sharp
relevance at the time. However, through that original
specific grounding, these words of God have an enduring
quality that continues to speak authoritatively and
relevantly. So we can read words that God spoke through
Moses at Mount Sinai more than a thousand years before
Christ, or words he spoke in Jerusalem through Isaiah and
Jeremiah, seven or eight centuries before Christ, or words
written by Paul to new believers in Corinth a few decades
after Christ – and we can still hear God speaking right into
our hearts today, when we learn how to listen properly.
That is what the Psalmist is observing. So even though he
probably lived centuries after the original giving of the
law, he affirms its abiding and universal relevance.

Another Psalmist said that God's law was more
precious than gold and sweeter than honey (Ps. 19). This
one might have changed the phrase 'diamonds are
forever' to 'God's word is forever.'

## ITS RIGHTEOUS QUALITY, OR MORALITY

The law not only shares God's eternal and universal
nature, it also reflects God's moral character, his
righteousness, justice, integrity and compassion. And it

does so fully, objectively and purposefully. Again, read these groups of verses and reflect on their affirmations and the Psalmist's response.

> Righteous are you, O LORD,
>     and your laws are right.
> The statutes you have laid down are righteous;
>     they are fully trustworthy (vv137-138).

● *What is the link between being right and being trustworthy? How does this work in everyday life (e.g. clocks, scales)? How does this affect our trust in God's moral teaching in Scripture?*

> ... because I consider all your precepts right,
>     I hate every wrong path (v128).

> Your statutes are for ever right;
>     give me understanding that I may live (v144).

> May my tongue sing of your word,
>     for all your commands are righteous (v172).

● *What are the personal responses that the Psalmist makes in response to his knowledge that God's law is morally perfect?*
● *How can we emulate them in our lives in relation to God's word? Think about the balance that is expressed between moral effort (v128) and hearty singing (v172).*

In Hebrew the word for righteous is *saddiq*. The noun for righteousness or justice is *sedeq* or *sedaqah*. Part of their meaning refers to something that is truly what it is supposed to be, setting the standard or norm by which everything else can be measured. In the context of this psalm it is God's word and God's law that provides the standard by which our behaviour is measured. They are the straight edge or the plumb line. This is where we bring all our ethical opinions and choices for testing.

So it is because God's law is righteous that it is trustworthy (think of accurate weights and measures) and it is because God himself is righteous, that his word shares the same moral quality.

● *Think back over the last year. When has a passage of Scripture functioned like a 'straight edge' in your life, setting an ethical standard of righteousness for your attitude or behaviour in some situation? Is there a passage of Scripture that is doing this right now?*

## ITS TRUTH, OR REALITY

*Read verses 142, 151 and 160.*

> Your righteousness is everlasting
>   and your law is true (v142).

> Yet you are near, O LORD,
>   and all your commands are true (v151).

> All your words are true;
>   all your righteous laws are eternal (v160).

● *These verses take three of the eight words used for God's law (see introduction, page xiii) and make the same affirmation about all of them: they are true. Check this for yourself. Read the preceding verses in each of the quoted sections. What do they show about the circumstances of the Psalmist?*

● *How should our confidence in the truth of God's word
sustain us in difficult times? Can you give examples of
when it has done so?*

Verse 160 literally says 'the sum, or the totality, of your
words is true'. It is not so much thinking of every word as
true, as saying that the full revelation of God in the
comprehensive wholeness of his words to us constitutes
the truth, and so can be trusted forever.

Truth is that which corresponds to reality. Truth is the
faithful reflection of what is objectively the case. A statement
can only be true (or false) if it refers to something real. That
is to say, it has to be referential and verifiable. For example,
if I make the statement 'Sea water is salty' it can be claimed
as true because of the objective reality of the sea and its
mineral content. But if I say, 'Tooth fairies have wings' it is
neither true nor false (except within the imaginary
framework of, say, a child's picture book), for there is no
objective reality (tooth fairies) to which it relates.[1]

So if we say 'The word of God is true' we mean that it
refers to reality – the ultimate reality of God and his
capacity to communicate. We also mean that all that God's
word itself refers to is part of reality. It communicates to us
the reality of the creation, of our human life in the image
of God, of our sin and brokenness, of God's action in
history for the redemption of humanity and all creation.
These things are real. This is the way it really is. This is
how we came to be where we are, and this is how God
intends to take things to where he plans.

So when this Psalmist makes these great claims for the
word of God, he means a lot more than factual accuracy.
He means that this word is where he finds a truthful,
dependable account of what is 'really real'. And that is
what he then builds all his life and hope upon. Anything
else is sinking sand.

Putting our three points together then, our Psalmist looks at the word of God, and makes it the object of his total trust. That is to say, he sees it as a solid, objective, dependable reality.

- *It is universal in its scope and relevance*
- *it is normative in its moral measurements and demands*
- *it is reliable in its truth claims*

The word of God is, for this Psalmist, the ultimate reference point for his metaphysics, for his ethics and for his epistemology.

Now these are vast claims. And they are controversial claims too in the context of the contemporary surrounding culture and ethos of postmodernity – in the West at least. The postmodern assertion is that there is no transcendent, eternal reality, no objective universal morality, and no absolute or final truth. The search for such certainties – through religion, or philosophy, or even through science, is misguided, pointless and oppressive. No culture, no religion, no ideology (including the myth of scientific progress) embodies universally valid truth in its narratives, demands, promises or morals. All is relative. Everything ebbs and flows in the great tides of history and culture. Life is a carnival – enjoy the variety and plurality as it passes by, but don't look for depth or ultimate foundations. There are none. There is no ultimate reality – only image. There is no ultimate morality – only what is good for you. There is no ultimate eternity – only the surface experience of the present.

What does Psalm 119 have to say in response? The affirmation of this Psalm is that:

- *There* is *an eternal transcendent reality – the living, personal Creator and Redeemer God, and we have access to him through his word.*

● *There* is *a universally relevant moral standard that claims all human beings in every age and culture; we have access to it through God's word, though he has planted the awareness of it in all people made in his own image (see Romans 1:19-20).*

● *There* is *an objective truth – an account, an explanation, a worldview, which faithfully corresponds to the way things really are, and we have access to as much of it as we can grasp.*

Our acceptance of this worldview, like all human knowing, is based on faith – reasonable, warranted faith. You can stand on and defend this faith; it is one upon which you can build your life, choices and future.

That is where this Psalmist stands as he articulates his convictions and his commitments. God's word is the focus of his faith. Is that where we stand too?

---

**FURTHER STUDY**

Read Leviticus 5:14-19, 25:8-31, Numbers 14:3-21 and 1 Corinthians 11:4-10 for starters. How do we go about finding and applying the abiding relevance and authority of different passages of the Bible, which were not originally written to us? You may be able to think of some other passages too.

In what way do we move from their specific context, through the wider intention of God embodied in them, to our own specific context? Try and list some examples of how that works.

**REFLECTION AND RESPONSE**

Jesus is God's living word (see Jn. 1), and he claimed to be 'the way, and the truth and the life' (Jn. 14:6).

What aspects of the word of God, highlighted in the study above, are filled out and made personal in Jesus, and how does that affect the way we combine our Bible reading with our relationship with Christ and our obedience to him?

# CHAPTER 2

# God's word as the focus of love and obedience

*Aim: To examine the strength of our emotional and obedient response to God's word*

The Psalmist simply *revels* in God's word. He uses all kinds of colourful, warm and emotional language about it, and he does this most often precisely when he is talking about God's law. This may come as a shock to those who thought that the Old Testament was all about legalism and cold obedience to external codes. In this chapter we will see how God's law is a joy and a delight, the object of love and very precious.

## GOD'S LAW AS A JOY AND A DELIGHT

*Read verses 14 and 162.*

> I rejoice in following your statutes
>    as one rejoices in great riches (v14).

> I rejoice in your promise
>> like one who finds great spoil (v162).

● *Joy, enjoy, enjoyable, rejoicing. In what contexts do we use these words?*

● *How does the Psalmist use the words? What does this tell us about his attitude to God's law?*

*Read verses 16, 24, 35 and 47.*

> I delight in your decrees;
>> I will not neglect your word (v16).

> Your statutes are my delight;
>> they are my counsellors (v24).

> Direct me in the paths of your commands,
>> for there I find delight (v35).

> For I delight in your commands
>> because I love them (v47).

● *Delight, delighted, delightful; reflect on the ways that you use these words in everyday speech. What circumstances and situations produce this reaction?*

● *What in practice could it mean to delight in God's commands?*

Read the rest of these 'delight' passages, looking also at the immediate context of each verse in your Bible.

> Their hearts are callous and unfeeling,
>> but I delight in your law (v70).

If your law had not been my delight,
    I would have perished in my affliction (v92).

Trouble and distress have come upon me,
    but your commands are my delight (v143).

I long for your salvation, O LORD,
    and your law is my delight (v174).

- *What contrast is there between the expressions of delight
  and the surrounding realities that the Psalmist was facing?*
- *Can you testify to a time when verse 143 was true for you?*

## GOD'S LAW AS THE OBJECT OF LOVE

While we may use the language of delight on a regular basis, we are somewhat more careful about who or what we apply the word 'love' to. The language of love is not at all out of place, however, when the Psalmist thinks of God's law. In fact, he emphasises it.

I lift up my hands to your
    commands, which I love . . . (v48).

Oh how I love your law!
    I meditate on it all day long (v97).

I hate double-minded men,
    but I love your law (v113).

I open my mouth and pant,
    longing for your commands (v131).

The language is emotive and expressive, and even physical in its longing (v131). This is the same verb (*'ahab*) that is used for loving God, loving our neighbour, loving a spouse, etc.

● *How should this affect our attitude to God's word?*
  *Can we assent to what the Psalmist says in verse 131?*

*Turn to verses 140, 163, 165 and 167.* What is the particular benefit that verse 165 affirms for loving God's law? How different is this from a 'burden of legalism'?

Of course, if you truly love someone, you don't forget them. So we could include as a sub-set of this 'love' theme a group of texts in which the Psalmist says he will never forget God's law either. Of course he won't – he loves it too much for that.

● *You don't forget a loved one even when you are far away*
  *from home, or in the middle of the night (vv54-55). A few*
  *summers ago, my wife spent two weeks in Canada for a*
  *family wedding. I was unable to go, for work reasons. It was*
  *an unusual experience for her to be the one travelling and*
  *me to be the one left at home. But did we forget each other?*
  *Of course not. Last thing at night and first thing in the*
  *morning I put my head on her pillow and prayed for her*
  *(though I can't say that I rose at midnight to give her*
  *thanks, v62!).*
● *The Psalmist would not forget God's words even in the face*
  *of opposition (v61) or danger (v109). On the contrary, they*
  *are what have saved him in the past (v93) and he trusts will*
  *help him find his way in the present and future (v176).*
● *What tends to make us forget God's word? And what*
  *happens when we do?*

## GOD'S LAW AS SUPERBLY PRECIOUS

The law is something so valuable, so precious, so endearing to the Psalmist that it can only be described in superlatives.

● *What is the most valuable thing you can think of? Gold? Silver? God's law is more precious than either.*

The law from your mouth is more precious to me
than thousands of pieces of silver and gold (v72).

. . . I love your commands more than gold,
more than pure gold (v127).

● *What is the sweetest thing you can think of? Honey? God's word tastes even better.*

How sweet are your words to my taste,
sweeter than honey to my mouth (v103).

Nothing is of more value than faithful obedience to God. Nothing is more satisfying than living according to his word. God's word, then, is not just the focus of intellectual assent and faith. It is also the focus of our emotional delight, love and appreciation.

So, as we summarize the three sections of this chapter, where is all this so-called Old Testament legalism referred to at the beginning of this chapter? Where is all this bondage to the law? It is tragic that even as Christians we have imbibed the cultural prejudice (which is actually as old as the fall of humanity in the Garden of Eden) that obedience is a negative word, implying loss of freedom. On the contrary, this Psalmist revels in the fact that, since

God's law was designed to enhance human life and well-being, obedience to God's law is the perfect recipe for true freedom, whether life is portrayed as running along a path, or walking around in open spaces.

> I run in the path of your commands,
>     for you have set my heart free (v32).

> I will walk about in freedom,
>     for I have sought out your precepts (v45).

● *How does the Psalmist's claim to hold God's law in the number one position challenge the subconscious priorities that govern our everyday lives?*

## GOD'S LAW AS REQUIRING OBEDIENCE

The word (especially the law) of God is a matter of intellectual assent. The Psalmist *believes it* (chapter 1). It is also for emotional appreciation. The Psalmist *loves it*. But it goes further than both the mind and the emotions. God's word is also there for volitional commitment. We must choose to *obey it*.

Think of what Jesus said in John 14:15: 'If you love me, you will obey what I command.' The Psalmist will have heard something similar, since the book of Deuteronomy emphasizes both love for God and obedience to his law in virtually the same breath (e.g. Deut. 6:4-9; 30:2,6,10). So the Psalmist determines to put God's law into practice as a matter of constant, deliberate, willing choice. It must shape the way he thinks and lives. Heads, hearts and hands, as we said at the outset.

## 'With all my heart'

The Psalmist uses the expression 'with all my heart' about eight times, stressing his total personal commitment to obeying God's law. This, after all, was how Deuteronomy had summarized the primary responsibility of all Israelites, in the great affirmation and exhortation of the *Shema'*.

> Hear O Israel: The LORD our God, the LORD is one. Love the LORD your God with all your heart and with all your soul and with all your strength (Deut. 6:4-5).

But why did we not include this point in our last section about love, the more emotional response to God and his word? Surely 'love with all your heart' is emotional language? Well, not entirely. The word 'heart' in Hebrew was not so much the seat of your emotions as the seat of your will. Emotions tended to be located lower down the body – in the bowels, for example – where you felt pity, compassion, tenderness. The heart, for an Israelite, was where you did your thinking. The heart was where you made your decisions and choices. The heart was what governed your intentions and planning. The heart, in other words, was the source of your actual conduct – for good or ill. That is why Jesus could say, 'out of men's hearts come evil thoughts, sexual immorality, theft, murder, adultery, greed, malice, deceit, lewdness, envy, slander, arrogance and folly' (Mk. 7:21-22). In this he echoed the original verdict on the human heart in Genesis 6:5. You need to watch your heart if you want to change your behaviour.

But for this Psalmist, the law of God was what he wanted to govern his heart, so he puts his whole heart into it. Read the 'heart-beat' verses below and consider the different things that the Psalmist says he will do with all his heart, or what he has set his heart on. How does that apply to your own choices and actions?

> Blessed are they who keep his statutes
>   and seek him with all their heart (v2).

> I seek you with all my heart,
>   do not let me stray from your commands (v10).

> I have chosen the way of truth;
>   I have set my heart on your laws (v30).

> Give me understanding, and I will keep your law
>   and obey it with all my heart (v34).

> Turn my heart towards your statutes
>   and not towards selfish gain (v36).

> I have sought your face with all my heart;
>   be gracious to me according to your promise (v58).

> My heart is set on keeping your decrees
>   to the very end (v112).

> I call with all my heart; answer me, O LORD,
>   and I will obey your decrees (v145).

### 'Fully, forever and now'

Shallow obedience is one of the things that Jesus both warned and complained about. This Psalmist wants none of it. He has a great determination that his commitment to God and his word will be total and lasting.

*Read the following verses*

Oh that my ways were steadfast
    in obeying your decrees! (v5).

My soul is consumed with longing
    for your law at all times (v20).

I will always obey your law,
    for ever and ever (v44).

● *What does the word choice mean in today's world?*
*Cappuccino today, espresso tomorrow? Choices can change*
*with tastes or fashions. In verse 60 we read that the Psalmist*
*'will hasten and* not delay *to obey your commands'. What*
*kind of commitments have you made, if any, that match the*
*language of 'at all times', 'for ever and ever'?*

There is no point in promising something 'forever' if it
doesn't include 'today'.

---

### FURTHER STUDY

What did Jesus say about our priorities? Think of some of the sayings
of Jesus about the kingdom of God as the supreme value, priority,
and 'prize' in life; and about what matters most in life. You may
want to read Matthew 13:31-52 for starters.

### REFLECTION AND RESPONSE

• Think about the culture and ethos of the particular Christian
group that you belong to (your church, or denomination, or
favourite Christian gathering or festival).

• Does it exhibit the balance of the three things we have studied
above – solid teaching for the mind; healthy enthusiasm for the
emotions and clear moral guidelines for biblical obedience?

• If not, where does the imbalance lie and what could you do to
correct it?

## CONCLUSION TO SECTION ONE

The two studies in this section surely throw out a challenge to us all to check out the health and strength of our personal commitment to the word of God in our lives. I think it particularly speaks to those of the present generation most affected by the culture of postmodernity – especially in the West. There is a lot about the postmodern shift that is welcome and friendly to the gospel. We may indeed welcome its greater emphasis on

- *the narrative dimension of life (we all love stories, and live out our stories)*
- *the significance of the local and cultural context in which we live*
- *the value of all cultures and the need to overcome our innate ethno-centrism*
- *relational rather than merely individualistic ways of thinking and living*
- *resistance to totalizing and oppressive powers*

However, when postmodern culture also denies *any* absolute foundations, *any* ultimate truth, *any* non-negotiable objective reality, *any* universally valid moral standards then we must challenge it at a fundamental worldview level. Can you build the foundations of your life on a swamp or a moving walkway?

## HERE IN PSALM 119 WE ARE IN THE COMPANY OF SOMEONE WHO IS

a) Intellectually convinced about God's word: its eternal transcendence, moral value and final truth;

b) Emotionally excited about God's word, finding it to be the object of delight, love and highest priorities;

c) Whole-heartedly committed to obeying God's word in the whole of life.

All three of the above are needed to work together for radical and balanced Christian discipleship and obedience.

Think about what a) can become without b) and c). It can produce dry intellectual, academic sterility – doctrinal soundness with no life, warmth or practical outworking.

Think about what b) without a) and c) can become. It can degenerate into frothy emotionalism and excitement, with no depth of understanding; or into the hypocrisy of enthusiasm without genuine practical obedience.

Think about what c) without a) and b) can be like. It can explode into zeal without knowledge, hasty and enthusiastic action without wisdom; it may eventually perish in disillusionment or arid legalism, when the love and joy are lost. Are we balanced Christians?

# Personal Guidance and the Word of Light

**Recommended reading:
Psalm 119:97-104, 105**

# Personal Guidance and the Word of Light

## INTRODUCTION TO SECTION 2

'Onward Christian soldiers, marching as to war.' The old hymn is not sung as much as it used to be. But some of us like the different beat of 'marching in the light of God'. Such songs conjure up the picture of a glorious army moving forward, in step, in time, in perfect formation (though they can only ever do so on the parade ground of course, not in actual battle). Well, it is a biblical picture, though it has to be said that it is more often applied to God in action than to the people of God.

In reality, life is more often described in the Bible, not so much as marching like an army, but simply as walking purposefully along a path. But for some of us, life may feel more like lurching unsteadily from one crisis to another, or wandering in increasing mystification through a maze of dead ends and blind choices.

We all long for clear guidance. Why else are horoscopes so popular? And as Christians we long to know 'what God would have us do'. We sometimes wish he would tell us clearly. Sometimes we think he has told us for certain, and then things don't turn out as we thought they should do if he really had. We would like to be wise and discerning in the choices we make. We really do want to do God's will and follow his plan for our lives.

Well, so did this Psalmist. He clearly not only wants to avoid sinning, or making disastrous mistakes. He wants more than God's help and protection in his struggles. He wants to live well in every sense of that word. His ambition is to be *wise* (intellectually), *godly* (spiritually) and *moral* (practically) in all the everyday things of life. And so he repeatedly asks God for two things:

- *Light for the path* – or guidance in his decisions.
- *Learning for the pupil* – or discernment in his thinking.

These will be the topics for the two chapters in this section.

CHAPTER 3

# Light for the path

*Aim: To reconsider what the Bible means by God's guidance in our lives*

**FOCUS ON THE THEME**
What have been some of the choices and decisions that you have made in the last year? It could be moving house, applying for university, buying a new car, going on a short-term mission. How did you make these decisions? To what extent do we include God in our plans?

The psalm begins with this familiar biblical metaphor for life.

> Blessed are they whose ways are blameless,
>    who *walk* according to the law of the LORD (v1).

A path that we walk along, a way that we follow, or a journey we undertake, is frequently used in the Bible to describe the course of a person's life, conduct, choices and actions. We still use it. We speak of having a career path or a way of life; or someone 'goes off the tracks'. And we like to think and sing and pray concerning our 'walk with the Lord'. Life is a journey.

The Psalmist frequently brings his way or ways before God as a matter of concern or intention. *Read verses 29, 32 and 59. What immediate impression do you gain from these verses about the way the Psalmist wanted his life to be?*

Keep me from deceitful ways;
  be gracious to me through your law (v29).

I have chosen the way of truth;
  I have set my heart on your laws (v30).

I run in the path of your commands,
  for you have set my heart free (v32).

I have considered my ways
  and have turned my steps to your statutes (v59).

- *Scan quickly through the rest of the psalm and find examples of other verses where the language of walking, running, feet, steps, way or path occurs.*
- *What does this tell us about the way the Psalmist wanted to live? Can we say the same about ourselves?*

## WALKING IN THE WAY OF THE LORD

An early example of this expression goes back to Abraham. In the context of the wicked way of Sodom, God reminds himself that he had chosen Abraham to walk in a different way.

I have chosen him, so that he will direct his children and his household after him to keep the way of the LORD by doing what is right and just, so that the LORD will bring about for Abraham what he has promised him (Gen. 18:19).

The way of the LORD involves doing righteousness and justice (two of the biggest words in the ethical vocabulary of the Old Testament). And this was to be characteristic of the people descended from Abraham – namely Israel. The mission of Israel was to walk in the way of the LORD, so that God could thereby bless the nations.

Another helpful example of the expression comes in Deuteronomy.

> And now, O Israel, what does the LORD your God ask of you but to fear the LORD your God, *to walk in all his ways*, to love him, to serve the LORD your God with all your heart and with all your soul, and to observe the LORD's commands and decrees that I am giving you today for your own good? (Deut. 10:12-13, italics mine).

This phrase comes in a group of five items. It is like a great single harmonic chord, composed of five distinct notes. What does God require? Only that we should fear, walk, love, serve and obey. In other words, above and beyond all the details of the surrounding laws in Deuteronomy, God is looking for the life commitment that these words embody.

But what does it mean to walk in the ways of the LORD? What are his ways that we should walk in them? The answer comes in the following verses, after some noisy doxology:

> For the LORD your God is God of gods and Lord of Lords, the great God, mighty and awesome, who shows no partiality and accepts no bribes. He defends the cause of the fatherless and the widow, and loves the alien, giving him food and clothing. And you are to love those who are aliens, for you yourselves were aliens in Egypt (Deut. 10:17-19).

The character of God is one of integrity, compassion, justice and practical care for the marginalized. Therefore, to walk in his ways means to imitate these qualities in him.

And those who are careful to walk in this way of life portrayed in God's covenant law can enjoy the promise of God's continued blessing. And this is the same dynamic that we find in the first verse of our psalm, as indeed in the opening psalm of the whole book.

> Blessed is the man who does not walk in the counsel
> of the wicked . . .
> For the LORD watches over the way of the righteous,
> but the way of the wicked will perish (Ps. 1:1,6).

## WATCHING YOUR WAY WITH THE WORD OF GOD

It's all very well for God to watch the path of the righteous, but how can we watch our own path? How am I to keep walking in the way of the LORD, when there are so many attractive alternatives and side-paths? That is a question the Psalmist himself asked – and answered:

> How can a young man keep his way pure?
> By watching it according to your word.
> (v9, my paraphrase)

It is God's word that provides the necessary light to show the right path we need to take. So we watch our footsteps with the help of God's word. It is light for the path. The Psalmist goes on to say 'Your word is a lamp to my feet and a light for my path' in what is a familiar and favourite verse to many (v105).

● *Think of a typical week – in work or at university, at home or wherever you may be. How can you work at 'watching your way' in the light of God's word? How will this affect the things that you do?*

## GUIDANCE AND THE BIBLE

There are innumerable books offering us guidance on everything from how to live a successful Christian life, to how to diet for Jesus (*What Would Jesus Eat?*), or how to train your dog the scriptural way (seriously – I have seen those books). Hints and tips for guidance are there for the taking – well, for the buying at least. Clearly somebody is making plenty of money out of our anxieties.

It is worth remembering that in the plethora of these *How to* books (with their ten easy steps to this or that spiritual achievement) your greatest resource in the matter of guidance is in your hand. It's the Bible itself. It is not a horoscope or a crystal ball. But it does offer guidance – rightly used and on its own terms. And the Bible should not be just in our hands. As Moses put it, 'No, the word is very near you; it is in your mouth and in your heart so you may obey it' (Deut. 30:14).

The Lord guides those who have his word stored in their hearts and on their lips, and who are committed to obeying it. This is different from shallow or mechanistic ways of trying to use the Bible. We have all heard about what happens when you stick a pin in a verse at random and hope it will give you a message. First stab: 'Judas went and hanged himself.' Second stab: 'Go and do thou likewise.' But one often comes across sincere Christians whose attempts at gaining God's guidance seem not much of an advance on that.

At All Nations Christian College there was a student who said that she was sure God had called her to mission in Latin America because she prayed to God to guide her; when she went into a shop that same day, the first thing she saw was a big bag of Brazil nuts. David Harley, my predecessor as Principal, said that he often wondered where she might have felt called to if she had spotted the Mars bars!

Shortly before my family and I left Britain for India where I was to teach the Old Testament at the Union Biblical Seminary, we had some natural anxieties about the huge transition we were making and about our impending journey to a strange land. In a prayer meeting a sincere brother 'shared a word from God' with my wife. It was God's word to Jacob to overcome his fears about going to Egypt (which must obviously have meant India for us). 'Do not be afraid to go down to Egypt, for I will . . . go down to Egypt with you, and I will surely bring you back again' (Gen. 46:3-4). God would go with us. God would bring us back. The brother meant well. I waited until later in the day before pointing out to Liz that the way God kept his promise to bring Jacob back from Egypt was in a coffin. That was not quite the kind of mummy she was hoping to be. Somehow the resolution of our anxieties in relation to God's guidance and providence needed a somewhat broader hermeneutical foundation. We need to study the whole of the Bible, and understand sound principles of interpretation and application for our lives.

Get to know your Bible in depth and as a whole, so that it seeps into your bloodstream. The Bible should not only be the object of our study, but also the subject of our thinking. That is, it is not what we think *about*, but what we think *with*. As Paul put it, 'Let the word of Christ dwell in you richly' (Col. 3:16).

In what ways does the Bible help us to discern God's guidance and to keep walking in his ways? Here are some of the ways that occurred to me. Perhaps you can think of others.

● *The Bible gives us access to the mind and values of God. Whatever decisions we come to should reflect his preferences in general, even when he gives no detailed guidance. The longer you spend in someone else's company, the more you get to know what their thoughts, feelings, likes, dislikes and preferences are. In the Bible, God has poured himself out to us: his heart, mind, priorities, plans and moral scale of values. Spend time reading the Bible. The more we do, the more our own thought processes and decision-making will be shaped by the mind of God.*

● *Constant exposure to the Bible sharpens our own value system, through its powerful stories, models, examples and direct teaching, and so informs the moral choices we have to make. Most of us have mental pictures or models of what constitutes a 'good' driver or teacher or parent. These are built up out of hundreds of stories, examples and personal experiences; from these we construct our archetype of such people – even if the real ones we know (including ourselves) fall rather short of the ideal. Similarly, it is from the multiplicity of stories in the Bible – positive and negative, inspiring and disturbing, that God shapes our instinctive perceptions of what is right and good in different circumstances and relationships.*

● *Similarly, the Bible sharpens our sense of sin and gives us clear warnings, in teaching and story, of what sin ends up doing to us. So we become more sensitive to the potential outcomes of different possible courses of action. (See 1 Cor. 10:1-13 for how Paul highlights this particular aspect of the Bible's function.)*

● *The Bible provides good soil for the work of the Holy Spirit in our minds. A mind that is already well soaked in the Scriptures will be one that is more in tune with the Spirit's leading.*

Can anyone in the group give specific examples of how the Bible has functioned effectively in guiding particular decisions or actions in the past?

## GUIDANCE OR BLUEPRINTS?

It is interesting to note that when the Psalmist is talking about God's guidance for his path it is framed more in the negative – i.e. avoiding wrong paths – than the positive (the *only* possible right way).

Take a look at some examples.

> because I consider all your precepts right,
>   I hate every wrong path (v128).

> I have kept my feet from every evil path
>   so that I might obey your word (v101).

> I gain understanding from your precepts;
>   therefore I hate every wrong path (v104).

The Psalmist seems to have been a relatively young person in a position of public leadership. Such responsibility could have brought many temptations.

● *What comparable wrong paths should we hate and 'keep our feet from' today? Are there are any paths we need to turn from now?*

The assumption seems to be that the Psalmist is already walking on a good path, simply by living as a faithful believer in obedience to God's word. But notice that he doesn't ask or expect that God will give him a detailed blueprint for every choice he has to make. He doesn't say, 'God, please show me what to do every day.' Certainly, it is the LORD's way he is walking in, but it is still 'my steps', 'my feet' and 'my path'. He still makes his own choices and decisions and looks for negative guidance – the red light or 'No Entry' sign, rather than positive guidance – 'Turn left here'.

We need to be careful about our theology of guidance. Many ideas that are common in Christian circles are not necessarily founded on a clear teaching of the Bible: 'God has a wonderful plan for your life.'[2] Or 'It's all mapped out to the last detail. So all you have to do is find it out. You're allowed as many questions as you like, but don't expect to get direct answers. And if you take a wrong step, you'll find yourself out of God's will, or at best, into second best, plan B.' I'm not at all sure that this is what the Bible means by God's sovereign purpose, or by God's promise to guide his people.

At the opposite extreme is the view that says, 'It's really entirely up to you. God has no more idea about what you will do with your life than you have. But if you make good choices, God will come alongside and help you through. He's as keen to find out what direction you take and where you end up as you are.' Again, I'm not at all convinced that this is an adequate way to describe the relationship between our free choices and the will of God. This approach is a distortion of what is indeed true biblical teaching about the openness of the future and the integrity of the personal and responsive relationship between God and people.

The first view gives us a sovereign God with a plan but leaves us groping around trying (and frequently failing) to get a fix on the details. The second view gives us a sovereign God without a plan and leaves us dangerously at sea without a rudder or compass. So what should we do?

The Bible certainly teaches that

- *God is sovereign over all that happens in the universe and over all history on earth*
- *God has a will and purpose that he is working out and will bring to final completion*
- *God promises to lead and guide his people*
- *God does lead and guide his people*

But there is little evidence in the Bible for the idea of an individualized blueprint, immutably fixed in advance, for every person's life, especially if it shades over into a more or less mechanical and fatalistic view of that plan. If the script is already written then it is easy to move to the implication that any deviation from this is like going off at a tangent – you will become farther and farther away from the original path you should have been on. Plan B is all you can settle for now. I remember George Verwer once saying that if this idea was true, he was glad there was a long alphabet, since he must be up to plan X or Y by now.

But is it like this? We know of course that David can speak of God's foreknowledge of his words and actions, and that all the days ordained for him were written in God's book (Ps. 139:3-4,16). But this probably speaks of intimate personal knowledge, and the length of time he would be alive rather than a detailed daily script fated to run its course, or a blueprint that had to be found out and followed. If so, David went about the matter in some strange ways.

There are two main problems that this blueprint model of guidance causes.

● *First, it can be the source of great pastoral damage and distress. Every now and then I have met someone who tells me their life story as a tale of woe. 'At the age of twenty-four I disobeyed God and missed his plan for my life, and I've been condemned to second best ever since.' Now undoubtedly people go astray and make a mess of their lives. But the God of the Bible is the God who is forever seeking to bring people back into restored relationship to himself, back to commissioning, service and fruitfulness. Think of Elijah. Think of Peter. He is the God who restores the years the locusts have eaten. He is the God who weaves even our mistakes and follies into his sovereign plan and 'in all things works for good of those who love him, who have been called according to his purpose' (Rom. 8:28). The blueprint model of guidance generates a great deal of unnecessary anxiety among some people who are desperately afraid they might miss some finer point of the future plan, and other people who are desperately afraid that they have already lost the plot somewhere in the past.*

● *Secondly, such a view of guidance reduces God to a heavenly puppeteer and reduces humanity to the level of animals that are controlled by mechanical means. In other words, it removes the personhood of God from his sovereignty, and removes the personhood of humanity from our decision-making. Both are serious misconceptions. God relates to us as our heavenly Father, not as our heavenly diary in advance. And it is part of the parenting process to bring your children to the maturity of making their own choices and decisions with wisdom and integrity. God has given us minds so we can think; consciences so that we can morally discriminate, and wills so that we can put our own plans into action. He expects us to use them, in prayerful conversation with him and in 'the fear of the Lord' – that is with the determination to do only what is consistent with his known character and general will.*

God's word then, to return to Psalm 119, is certainly a light for our path. But it does not pre-decide every step and every choice that we have to make. What we need, therefore, is not just light, so that we can see where we are going and avoid wrong or dangerous paths, but also discernment. We need that constantly maturing insight and understanding that will enable us to make wise and good decisions – decisions that are pleasing to God as well as being the best for ourselves and others. That too, is what the Psalmist prays for. And that is what we shall look at in the next chapter.

● *Think about people you know who are having to make big decisions. It could be a decision involving their family, job or home. Reflect on how they must be feeling and bring any particular prayer requests to your group. Then pray together for some of the people you have mentioned*

---

## FURTHER STUDY

Read Psalm 32. What is the clear promise that God makes in v8-9?

What is the first condition for being guided by God that is implied by the first part of the Psalm (vv1-7)?

What is the second condition that is expressed in v8-9?

If the difference between horses and mules on the one hand, and humans on the other, is that horses and mules 'have no understanding', what does this tell us about how God will guide us? And what does this verse tell us about how we should not expect God to guide us?

## REFLECTION AND RESPONSE

Review the last year. Can anyone in the group give specific examples of how the Bible has functioned effectively in guiding particular decisions or actions in the past?

# CHAPTER 4

# Learning for the pupil

*Aim: To assess our willingness to let God's word shape our thinking*

**FOCUS ON THE THEME**
Who have been the good teachers in your life? Why were they good? What difference did they make to your learning? Reflect on some of the qualities that you think make a good teacher.

There was a TV advert for teacher recruitment in the UK some years ago. It had a series of well known public faces appear (sports heroes, famous entertainers, leading politicians, etc.) and say the name of some otherwise unknown person: 'Mrs Jones', 'Mr Campbell', 'Miss Rutherford' and so on. Then the punch line of the advert would appear – *Nobody forgets a good teacher!* And it's true. We all remember the few really excellent teachers of our childhood days who made such an impact upon us. And this Psalmist remembers his teacher too – God. So the Psalmist often compares God to a teacher, and describes his word as teaching or instruction. And he frequently expresses his appreciation for having such a good teacher – as we all should, whether on a TV advert or not.

So the metaphor changes between the last chapter and this one. No longer are you thinking of taking a lamp along with you as you walk along a path on a dark night. Instead we are sitting with a teacher learning, studying, interacting, absorbing, memorizing, reflecting and applying what the teacher shares with us.

## GOD THE TEACHER

When the Bible is our textbook, then God himself is our teacher. Read verse 102:

> I have not departed from your laws,
>   *for you yourself have taught me* (v102 my italics).

This is how Paul also encouraged Timothy to think about his upbringing. Timothy had been well taught as a child by his mother and grandmother – and what a blessing and privilege. But Paul puts the emphasis on the Scriptures themselves as being what had led him to salvation and provided him with 'education in righteousness/justice'. As Paul writes in his second tetter to Timothy

> [H]ow from infancy you have known the holy Scriptures, which are able to make you wise for salvation through faith in Christ Jesus. All Scripture is God-breathed and is useful for teaching, rebuking, correcting and training in righteousness (2 Tim. 3:15-16).

Indeed, our Psalmist reckons that with God as his teacher and the Scriptures as his textbook, he has greater understanding than even his human teachers and elders (not to mention his enemies).

Verses 98-100 read

> Your commands make me wiser than my enemies,
>   for they are ever with me.

I have more insight than all my teachers,
   for I meditate on your statutes.
I have more understanding than the elders,
   for I obey your precepts.

● *If we are Christians, we believe with the Psalmist that the Bible gives greater insight and understanding than all other education. Why isn't this just anti-intellectualism?*

I would not accuse the Psalmist of arrogance in these claims, even though they could sound like the exaggerated confidence of youth. Rather, he is expressing confidence in the surpassing value and wisdom of the teaching of God in his word.

Perhaps you've heard of the university professor who told a new lecturer that if there was anything she didn't understand she should ask the first year students as soon as possible while they still knew everything about everything. It could be that a believing schoolchild who knows his or her Bible well may have greater understanding of God than a teacher with a theology degree.

Recently, I met up with someone from my Cambridge University days. She told me that her abiding memory of Hugh Williamson and me (we were theology students in the same year) was that we were constantly asking questions and challenging the theology lecturers. We sometimes thought they were talking rubbish. Maybe they were, but it was arrogant of us to think that we could put them right and that we were sure that we knew the Scriptures better than they did.

At least we know, or should know, better than to try that on with God himself, who teaches us through the Scriptures.

Working through the psalm with this thought in mind – of God as teacher and his word as our textbook – I discovered that two phrases cropped up: '*Teach me* your decrees' occurs eight times and 'Give me *understanding/ discernment*' (or a similar expression) is used seven times. So for the rest of the chapter let's look at these phrases in the context of the passages in which they occur. As we do we will find varying emphases – like the weaving of different threads in a tapestry. First of all we will see how the Psalmist's prayer to 'teach me' is linked with praise, practical life and obedience, and God's character and action.

## '*TEACH ME*'

1. Two of the times the Psalmist prays this, in fact the first and last time he does so, it is linked with *praise*:

   Praise be to you, O LORD;
       teach me your decrees (v12).

   May my lips overflow with praise,
       for you teach me your decrees (v171).

● *What are the more common things that we praise God for? Did anyone in the group mention his teaching? If not, or if it was not high on the list, what does this show about the priorities of our gratitude?*

For the Psalmist there was no dichotomy between his head and his heart, between theology and doxology, between the intellectual and the spiritual. He did not think of his worship in one box (praise and thanksgiving and singing) and teaching in another. No, his learning actually overflowed in praise (v171).

The same dynamic link between teaching and praise is found in Nehemiah 8. There we read that the people stood and listened to the law of God being read and taught to them for a whole week. And they wept. And then they rejoiced. And the main reason for their rejoicing was because, through the teaching work of the Levites, they now understood the words that were being read to them (Neh. 8:12). Paul makes a similar point in 1 Corinthians 14, when he urges believers not to get so carried away with their worship in the Spirit that they forget the importance of feeding the mind also (1 Cor. 14:14-19).

It is tragic when Christians separate devotional life, or so-called 'worship times', from learning and understanding God's word – or even set them over against each other in their thinking. Both are crucially important. This Psalmist longs to be taught so that he can worship and praise God better.

2. In verses 26-33 the Psalmist's prayer for God to teach him is linked to *practical life and obedience*.

> I recounted my ways and you answered me;
>   teach me your decrees (v26).

> Teach me, O LORD, to follow your decrees;
>   then I will keep them to the end (v33).

We sometimes talk about being accountable to each other for our words and actions. In verse 26 the Psalmist mentions his accountability to God. Do we give account at the end of each day? Discuss the way in which this might affect our motivation in studying Scripture.

3. Verses 64, 68, 124 and 135 show how the Psalmist's prayer is connected to *God's character and action.*

> The earth is filled with your love, O LORD;
>   teach me your decrees (v64).

> You are good, and what you do is good;
>   teach me your decrees (v68).

> Deal with your servant according to your love
>   and teach me your decrees (v124).

> Make your face shine upon your servant
>   and teach me your decrees (v135).

● *'Everybody remembers a good teacher.' The Psalmist wants to learn from this teacher because he is good, loving, and present with his pupil.*

● *The face of God means the presence of God, right there in the classroom. What difference should it make to our Bible study if we recall that it is carried on in the presence of our good and loving teacher?*

Many consider God's *law* as diametrically opposite to his *love*. In the Old Testament, however, God's law was considered one of the supreme gifts of God's grace to the people he loved and redeemed out of slavery. The idea then that study of the law was an exercise in arid legalism would have been utterly shocking to this Psalmist – it was nothing of the kind. It was an intimate, personal tutorial with his gracious divine teacher. The Psalmist is saying to God, 'Lord, I want *you*, you personally and you only, to be my teacher, because of your goodness, your love and your gracious personal presence with me.'

● *You, or your group, are involved in Bible study right now. God is your teacher, because it is his word you are studying. How can the Bible study result in praise, obedience and celebration of the character of God?*


## 'GIVE ME UNDERSTANDING'

'Understanding' in Hebrew means insight and discernment, seeing more deeply than your eyes can function. It is the ability to see behind the façade or beneath the surface. This is practical wisdom that comes with maturity and experience, but it can also be taught and learned to some degree – above all it is a gift of God that we should pray for. Indeed, in the New Testament it is among the gifts of the Spirit (1 Cor. 12:8).

Like the prayer that God would teach him, this prayer for understanding also involved the weaving together of threads to form a tapestry.[3] Here we will look at how this understanding is linked with God as Creator, moral obedience and a personal relationship with God.

1. Verses 27 and 73 link this request to *God as Creator*.

Let me understand the teaching of your precepts;
 then I will meditate on your wonders (v27).

Your hands made me and formed me;
 give me understanding to learn your commands (v73).

● *The suggestion here is that understanding God's moral teaching comes before reflection on his creation. What does this say about the relationship between religion/ethics and science?*

2. Understanding is linked to *moral obedience*, and especially avoiding wrong.

> Give me understanding, and I will keep your law
>   and obey it with all my heart (v34).

> I gain understanding from your precepts;
>   therefore I hate every wrong path (v104).

● *How has society perverted this priority by substituting intellectual and academic wisdom (or technological wizardry) for moral discernment?*

● *Can you give examples of times when your growth in Christian understanding helped you to reject and avoid making a wrong turn or decision?*

The whole point of *learning* from God is to *live* for God. Compare these verses with Proverbs 1:1-7.

3. Verses 125, 144 and 169 show how understanding is linked to *a personal relationship with God*.

> I am your servant; give me discernment
>   that I may understand your statutes (v125).

> Your statutes are for ever right;
>   give me understanding that I may live (v144).

> May my cry come before you, O LORD;
>   give me understanding according to your word (v169).

These verses underline a point I made in the introduction. This is not a psalm about the law itself, but about a personal relationship with God. The Psalmist's longing for growth in understanding – for intellectual and moral discernment – flows from his relationship with God. God, in these verses, is his Master, his Life-giver and his Helper. The Psalmist is simply God's servant. He needs God to give him life and he is needy enough to cry out for help.

● *What part does humility play in the gaining of biblical understanding?*

### FURTHER STUDY
Read 1 Corinthians 1:24-30. How does the Psalmist's longing for teaching and understanding relate to Paul's personalizing of all wisdom as being available to us through our relationship with God in Christ?

### REFLECTION AND RESPONSE
Why is it misleading, after a sermon, to use phrases such as 'And now the band is going to lead us into a time of worship'? What does this imply? What has this psalm taught you about how we should view worship? Conclude this study by spending some time in prayer, worshipping God for who he is and what he has done.

# Personal Sin
# and the Word of Grace

**Recommended reading: Psalm 119:9-16**

# Personal Sin and the Word of Grace

## INTRODUCTION TO SECTION 3

If you know the story of *Pilgrim's Progress*, you'll remember how Christian begins his journey carrying a terribly heavy burden of sin strapped to his back, longing to be rid of it. He struggles on through various kinds of terrain until he eventually comes to the foot of the cross, and there in a dramatic moment, his burden of sin falls off and rolls away down a great hole, never to be seen again.

Some of the psalms depict the weight of sin very heavily. The writer of Psalm 32, for example, vividly describes how his life had felt dry, crushed and wasted for as long as he lived with unconfessed sin in his life. When he tried to cover it up inside himself, it consumed him. When he uncovered it to God, then God could cover it with his forgiving grace.

Psalm 51 is probably the most extended confession of sin in the whole book, containing profound reflections, deep penitence and searching prayers for cleansing and restoration.

Psalms like these arise out of profound conviction, usually in the wake of some specific sin. They sigh in contrition and brokenness of spirit. Such times are excruciatingly painful, but by God's grace they can also be wonderfully restoring and filled with fresh hope. Godly repentance leads to God's forgiveness, and there is inexpressible joy in belonging to the fellowship of the forgiven.

Even though Psalm 119 is not really a confession psalm, that is not to say that it is not concerned about sin. The writer is not desperately sorry because he *has* sinned; he is desperately anxious that he *should not* sin. Perhaps this concern arises out of earlier experiences, similar to those that lie behind Psalms 32 and 51. Knowing what it had been like to be on his face under the anger of God, crying out for mercy and wishing more than anything to undo the past, he is determined not to end up there again. So what we find in this psalm is not so much a *confession* of sin as a *consciousness* of sin and a strong determination to do all he can to avoid it.

In the chapters of this section we shall look at the Psalmist's awareness of sin and what it does to you; at his strategy for the avoidance of sin; and at the remarkable answer to sin that we find from this Old Testament believer who knew nothing about Jesus and the cross.

# CHAPTER 5

# Awareness of sin

*Aim: To deepen our awareness of the effects of sin in our lives*

**FOCUS ON THE THEME**
Read Matthew 18:7-9. How do we view our sins? Do we try and justify 'small' sins? Come before God at the start of the chapter and ask him to increase your sensitivity to sin.

How does the Psalmist assess the seriousness of sin? What does it do to people? In this chapter we are going to look at awareness of sin under three headings: the awareness that sin leads to shame and disgrace, sin leads you astray, and sin eventually rules and dominates our lives. As we begin, reflect on the verses in the sections below. Is God speaking directly to you about a particular area in your life?

## 1. SIN LEADS TO SHAME AND DISGRACE

*Read verses 6, 31 and 39 below.*

Then I would not be put to shame
    when I consider all your commands (v6).

I hold fast to your statutes, O LORD;
    do not let me be put to shame (v31).

Take away the disgrace I dread,
    for your laws are good (v39).

We tend to associate shame with reports in the
newspapers of teachers who have been disgraced,
politicians who have been leading a double life or children
who have brought shame on the family name.

● *What kind of disgrace do you think the Psalmist is afraid of
and how is that relevant to us today?*

Shame is the first response to sin. In the Garden of Eden
Adam and Eve tried to cover themselves and to hide from
God. Shame is the urgent desire to be covered, to hide
away from the gaze of others. It happens when you are
found out, and the fear of being put to shame is great –
especially in some cultures where loss of face is
excruciating and something to be avoided at all costs.
Other psalms also express this fear of being put to shame.
Read, for example, Psalm 25:1-2,20. The Psalmist wants
God to protect him from public shaming that would come
about if he were falsely accused and people believed the
accusations.

But real sin (not just false accusation) should produce
shame. Even if not in public, there is a proper inward
shame that we ought to feel when we stand uncovered
before God and know our own hearts. It is when people
can sin without shame that they are in a serious spiritual
state of hardness.

Part of the suffering of crucifixion was the public shame
it inflicted on the victim. Normally, the victim was
crucified naked, making the public exposure even worse.
So the cross, for Jesus, involved not only bearing our sin
but also bearing our shame. That is to say, he took upon
himself the heaped up scorn, shame and abuse that should

have been ours. One of the two thieves recognized this, while the other simply joined in the abuse.

This dimension of the cross only impacted me when, on one occasion, I came to profound repentance for behaviour that had been well concealed; if it had come into the open it would have disgraced me. As I brought my sin to the cross for forgiveness, I suddenly realized that the shame I should and would have borne was indeed taken by Jesus. Not only did I find forgiveness and cleansing in the blood of Christ, but also protection from shame – just as the Psalmists prayed. It was deeply humbling and deeply reassuring.

> Bearing shame and scoffing rude
> *In my place* condemned He stood,
> Sealed my pardon with His blood
> Hallelujah! What a Saviour! (italics added)

### Shame in a 'sinless society'[4]

One of the shifts in our western postmodern culture is that the whole idea of sin has become fairly meaningless to many people. With the loss of any awareness of a transcendent personal God to whom we are morally accountable, there has been a corresponding loss of any sense of guilt in having offended him or having done wrong in some objective sense. In its place there is a sense of shame – but even that is not the same as the biblical sense of shame, namely shame in the presence of God. Rather, it is more an inner shame generated by a disconnection between the persona we project – the external image that is supported by the stories we tell of ourselves and the person we know ourselves to be on the inside. We are, literally, ashamed of ourselves.

One of the challenges facing us in communicating the liberating gospel of the Bible is how to respond to this cultural phenomenon. How do you think we should address the problem of the lack of a sense of sin, and the presence of a distorted sense of shame in our society? This may be a difficult and confusing topic to discuss as a group, but it is important to recognize that the familiar terminology we use as Christians in Bible studies may not make any sense in the world outside. How are we going to find ways of communicating the truth of what the Bible says in language and concepts that do make sense?

## 2. SIN LEADS YOU ASTRAY

We have already seen that one of the favourite pictures for the life of a believer in this psalm is that of a path, or a way. The Psalmist wants God to guide him in good and right ways. Equally, he wants to avoid taking the wrong path. And sin always puts you on the wrong path. When you deliberately do what you know is displeasing to God, it puts you on a wrong track – and that tends to lead to another wrong track (as you try to cover the first), and another, until you end up far away from where God wants you to be. Look at some of the verses where the Psalmist wants to avoid that fate.

> Before I was afflicted I went astray,
>   but now I obey your word (v67).

> I have kept my feet from every evil path
>   so that I might obey your word (v101).

● *In verse 67 the Psalmist suggests that his afflictions have stopped him going astray; now he is determined to be obedient. Can you think of any times in your own life when afflictions or sufferings have brought you back in line with God's word? Discuss these with the group.*

I gain understanding from your precepts;
   therefore I hate every wrong path (v104).

and because I consider all your precepts right,
   I hate every wrong path (v128).

● *'I hate every wrong path.' How can we cultivate this sort of attitude without becoming self-righteous as we do so?*

Wrong paths, of course, can also be dangerous paths. Once you know you are on a wrong path, the best thing to do is to turn back and retrace your steps. Sin always starts with one step; it then becomes a sequence of steps that lead you further down the wrong path. The further you go, the harder it becomes to turn back at all. So this Psalmist's wise advice is to do your best to avoid that first step.

## 3. SIN EVENTUALLY RULES AND DOMINATES YOUR LIFE

. . . just as God said it would do, in the Garden of Eden.

Sin becomes a hard master and we end up enslaved to it. Theological truth and personal experience match up at this point. As a friend of mine, experienced with helping drug abusers, says, 'When it comes to sin, we are all recovering addicts.' There is an addictive, dominating bondage in sin, which the Bible warns us about and from which only the power of God can first deliver us, and then protect us.

So one reason why our Psalmist prays for God to keep him on the right path is so that he will avoid being ruled and dominated by sin.

*Read verse 133 below.*

> Direct my footsteps according to your word;
>   let no sin rule over me.

● *What additional insights on this verse can you find in Romans 6:11-14?*

● *In what ways does the 'rule of sin' manifest itself in our lives?*

The Bible has a great deal more to say on the subject of sin in many other places – including other psalms. And reflection on our own experience as sinners should easily and quickly throw up many other ways in which we fall.

The Bible expects us to be realistic and radical in our attitude to sin. What are some of the things that sin claims to offer? I have listed some of these below.

● *Sin promises fun and excitement but it delivers pain and tragedy*

● *Sin promises freedom but it delivers slavery and addiction*

● *Sin promises life and fulfilment but it delivers emptiness, frustration and death*

● *Sin promises gain but it delivers loss*

● *Sin promises that we can get away with it, but the fact is, we don't*

Psalm 119 comes with a sober warning. Be aware of the reality of sin and what it does in human life. Acknowledge and face up to these things. Be real about yourself.

**FURTHER STUDY**
Read Psalm 51 prayerfully, asking God to renew and refresh you as David did. Are there particular areas in your life that you need to bring before God?

**REFLECTION AND RESPONSE**
Finish this chapter with the confession of sin and a thankfulness to God for the reality of his forgiveness in Christ. Sin is serious, but as Christians we know that ultimately our sin can be fully dealt with at the cross of Christ. Let this concluding thought shape your prayers and response to God now.

# CHAPTER 6

# Answering sin – through our minds and wills

---

*Aim: To strengthen our resistance to sin and our faith in God's mercy*

---

**FOCUS ON THE THEME**
Read Ephesians 6:10-18. Keep the battle imagery and the 'full armour of God' in mind as you read this chapter. You may want to return to this passage at the end of the study too.

How can we resist sin? The Bible tells us that sin radically and comprehensively affects the whole human person.

> The LORD saw how great man's wickedness on the earth had become, and that every inclination of the thoughts of his heart was only evil all the time (Gen. 6:5).

There is no part of the human personality that is uncorrupted by sin. Physical, spiritual, intellectual, emotional, intentional and relational dimensions of human life are all twisted and distorted by its infection.[5]

So if every part of our being is affected by sin, we have to engage every part of ourselves in resisting it. And that is exactly what we find the Psalmist doing. As we read his words, we can detect different emphases or tactics in his struggle to avoid temptation and sin. Let's analyse his strategy and see what it has to teach us in our own battles.

# 1. EXERCISING OUR MINDS

The psalm is filled, as we have seen again and again, with references to the word of God. And the writer tells us that he gives a lot of time and energy to exercising his mind on it – not just as an academic exercise, but with the specific purpose of avoiding sin and keeping his feet on the right path. In fact, he devotes the whole of the second section of the poem (vv9-16) to this, and begins with the question we are considering.

> How can a young man keep his way pure?
>   By living according to your word (v9).

The answer to the question is literally, '*By watching it, according to your word.*' It means bringing every step we make in life – every choice and decision, every opportunity or temptation – before the bar of God's word and asking 'What does the Bible say?'
*Read verses 11, 13 and 15.*

> I have hidden your word in my heart
>   that I might not sin against you (v11).

> With my lips I recount
>   all the laws that come from your mouth (v13).

> I meditate on your precepts
>   and consider your ways (v15).

Not only does the Psalmist recount God's laws, he also meditates and hides them in his heart. Discuss how we can meditate on God's word in our personal and group study. What does it involve?

Now we could skim through the psalm and doubtless find many more indications of the determination of this writer to give to the Scripture the serious mental attention it deserves. The Psalmist is clearly exercising his mind on God's word. He has not turned it into a few pious songs to soothe his heart. He is being diligent, systematic and industrious in his Bible study, and finding in it great joy and delight, which is as it should be.

- *Why does he give priority to studying God's law? He believes that by continually deepening his knowledge of the Scripture he will correspondingly strengthen his ability to avoid sinning. How does this work?*

- *Discuss, and illustrate from experience, one or two of the following factors that are at work in this dynamic, sin-disinfecting effect of Bible study*

- *Knowing the Bible keeps us more in touch with the mind of God. In turn we become more sensitive to sin. We are more alert to his priorities, not merely subject to the prejudices or legalism of the tradition we may belong to.*

- *The Bible provides many examples of the temptations that humans are exposed to. They are there for our benefit. We should be asking 'Is there an example to follow or an error to avoid?' Bible narratives have great teaching power as they shape our 'sin-sensors.'*

- *Having the Bible stored in your heart and mind gives you strong ammunition against temptation. Or to use Paul's metaphor, the word of God is 'the sword of the Spirit.' The more we fill our minds with Spirit-inspired Scriptures, the more we will be equipped for the battles ahead.*

- *The Bible is blunt and unflattering. It is 'sharper than a double-edged sword' (Heb. 4:12). One effect of that, in my experience at least, is that the Bible quickly snuffs out our* tendency to rationalize and excuse our own sin. As we come up with all kinds of reasons why we couldn't really help it, or why it is really somebody else's fault, the Bible sits there, convicting us: 'Who do you think you're kidding? Get real, my friend.' The Bible ruthlessly unmasks our pretence and sham.

– We think, 'I can get away with it; nobody knows.' And the Bible murmurs, 'Be sure . . . your sin will find you out' (Num. 32:23).

– We think, 'God doesn't really mind; he's too nice to make a fuss about what I'm doing.' And the Bible thunders with its awesome health warning, 'Do not be deceived: God cannot be mocked. A man reaps what he sows' (Gal. 6:7).

The more we instil the Bible into our heart, mind, soul and bloodstream, the harder we will find it to sin comfortably. The Bible enlivens our conscience and drives us back to God in repentance and a longing to live as it pleases him. Fill your mind with it as much as you can.

## 2. EXERCISING OUR WILLS

Psalm 119 resonates with determination. The Psalmist leaves us in no doubt as to what he *wills* to do and not do. He is going to choose to do what is good and choose not to do what is evil. We have no way of knowing how successful he may or may not have been in keeping his resolutions. He was human like the rest of us, so no doubt he failed pretty often. But the point is he was determined to avoid sin, and he knew he needed to strengthen his will in that direction, as well as exercising his mind on the word of God.

*Read the verses below*. Verse 30 displays a positive exercise of the will while verse 101 refers to the negative.

I have chosen the way of truth;
  I have set my heart on your laws (v30).

I have kept my feet from every evil path
  so that I might obey your word (v101).

● *Discuss what 'choosing the way of truth' means. How does this relate to your own personal experience and circumstances?*

● *Which would you say was more demanding: positive obedience or negative avoidance? Why?*

*Read verses 106 and 112 below.*

I have taken an oath and confirmed it,
  that I will follow your righteous laws (v106).

My heart is set on keeping your decrees
  to the very end (v112).

The will needs to have long-term goals in view otherwise it gets reduced to whims and fancies (e.g. 'What will you do today?'), which is what our postmodern culture is good at, including some very easygoing forms of Christian living within it. So to set your heart, i.e. your will, on something 'to the very end' is strongly counter-cultural.

● *In verse 106 the Psalmist talks about having taken an 'oath'. Can you think of an appropriate cultural equivalent for us?*

It is important to recognize that sin *is* a matter of choice and will. Yes, of course, it is also a matter of temptation, seduction, enticement and sometimes just stumbling over and falling down before we even see the trip-wire. But temptation is not compulsion.

The very first sin recorded in the Bible was an act of choice. Once the insidious conversation between the serpent and Eve had taken place, in which she had been led to question God's motives and doubt his goodness, the serpent plays no further part in the story until summoned by God for judgment. The serpent did not offer Eve a glass of freshly squeezed fruit juice and pour it down her throat.

She saw, she thought, she took, she ate, she gave and he ate also. Eve and Adam *chose* to disobey. They were not compelled to.

It may sound almost absurd, but the truth is, you don't have to sin. Let me clarify. In saying 'you don't have to sin', I do not mean that it is then possible for us to be sinless or morally perfect. We *do* sin. We are born into a legacy of sin. We are fallen in Adam and sin is part of our fallen human nature. In fact, as John puts it, if we say we do not sin, we are deceiving ourselves and calling God a liar as well (1 Jn. 1:8-10). But this inherent tendency towards sin does not remove our moral responsibility for the choices we make and the actions we do. The essence of sin is that indeed we do deliberately choose to do what we *know* we ought not to do, and not to do what we *know* we ought to do. This is a fact of experience that Paul wrestles with in Romans 7. It is a choice we make, not coercion. We are not robots or puppets on a string, or even merely animals acting on instinct. We are morally conscious human persons to whom God has given the gift of choosing, of exercising our own wills.

So for all these reasons, it is vital to strengthen our *wills* in the direction of God's will. Like this Psalmist we need to think, to decide, to take steps and to determine what we will and will not do.

Of course we all fail. But that does not mean there is no point in making the effort and praying for God to work within us to mould our will to his. The Holy Spirit is the gentle persuader, working within us so that we will what he wills; we choose what he would choose.

A biblical example may help here. What did Joseph do when faced with sexual temptation? He resisted first with explanatory words that showed where his priority and commitments lay – to his benefactor and master, Potiphar, and to his God (Gen. 39:7-9). His will in the matter was clear and reinforced 'day after day' (v10). So when the temptation was repeated with urgent physical appeal, he made an urgent physical exit (v12).

● *Read Daniel 1. How did Daniel and his friends resolve to honour God and at what cost?*

The earlier you take a stand, the stronger you become to face harder tests later. A young friend of mine is an accountant in training. A senior partner in the firm asked him to sign off some accounts that contained some irregularities. His conscience was stirred: he knew he couldn't agree to such work ethics. But if he refused, would it endanger his chances of success and a good reference for future employment? We talked about it and looked at the numerous Bible texts that speak of the supreme value that God puts on integrity and honesty, and the cost involved in living by that standard.[6]

Not all resolutions are so successful of course, and the Bible is honest in recording the failures as well as the successes. Peter, like all the disciples, said he would never deny Jesus but would die with him if necessary. All the other disciples forsook him and fled (except for Peter and John), and then Peter denied he even knew Jesus. His good resolutions had lasted about three hours. What a failure! But the answer to Peter's failure of will and nerve at that point lay in Jesus' restoring love and re-commissioning after the resurrection. Peter the failure became Peter the forgiven, and the same Peter, out of that experience, writes to the rest of us in his two epistles.

---

**FURTHER STUDY**

Read 1 Peter 5:8-10. What does Peter say we have to do and what does he promise that God will do? A parallel passage to consider is found in James 4:7-10.

Notice what we have to do and what Peter promises that God will do. Both involve our wills. We exercise them, God strengthens them.

**REFLECTION AND RESPONSE**

Have there been times when resisting temptation came down to sheer will-power and choosing against the odds to do the right thing? What was the cost? What was the result?

# CHAPTER 7

# Answering sin – through our emotions and faith

*Aim: To encourage our faith in God's compassion and mercy*

**FOCUS ON THE THEME**
Read the warning to the Church in Laodicea in Revelation 3:15-17. What lessons can we learn from this passage in relation to the way we view our sins? What are the dangers of being an emotional lukewarm Christian?

In chapter 6 we looked at how the challenge of avoiding sin includes exercising our *minds* on the word of God, and exercising our *wills* to bring our choices and actions into line with the will of God. But this Psalmist is not just a cold intellectual, with his head stuffed full of the Bible and sound doctrine. Nor is he just a cold disciplinarian, all buttoned up in the stern self-control of an iron will. On the contrary, he *feels* very deeply and does not hesitate to give full vent to some very strong emotions. In this chapter we will look at our response to sin through our emotions and faith.

## 1. EXERCISING OUR EMOTIONS

Among the Psalmist's strongest, deepest and most frequently expressed emotions is his reaction to sin and evil. As you read the verses below, use your own words to describe the emotions he feels.

Indignation grips me because of the wicked,
  who have forsaken your law (v53).

I gain understanding from your precepts;
  therefore I hate every wrong path (v104, see also v128).

I look on the faithless with loathing,
  for they do not obey your word (v158).

I hate and abhor falsehood
  but I love your law (v163).

Streams of tears flow from my eyes,
  for your law is not obeyed (v136).

Here are some strong emotions! Part of the reason for such strong feelings could be that the Psalmist's mind is so saturated with the Scriptures that he is echoing or mirroring some of the emotions of God himself towards sin. The prophets do the same thing. All the feelings of God come out in their words – his anger, grief, disbelief, disgust, sense of betrayal, frustration – even nostalgia for better times and longing for better things.

We may be inclined to wrinkle our noses in disapproval when we hear the Psalmist expressing such sentiments. But was he not right to feel that way about sin and evil, if God does? We are called to share God's hatred of wickedness without falling into hatred and abuse of the people involved. That is the difficulty. Ought we not to pray more that God would increase our sensitivity to our own sin?

It is when we find that we can sin without even batting an emotional eyelid that we have seriously lost touch with the heart of God. But if the word of God fills our hearts and minds, then our emotions will also be affected by the feelings of God's heart, and that will inevitably involve an emotional reaction of some kind to sin – in ourselves and in the world.

## 2. EXERCISING OUR FAITH

So does the psalm provide another popular DIY course in Christian spirituality: *Sin and How to Avoid It in Three Simple Steps*? For surely, all you've got to do is read your Bible every day, think positively and keep in touch with your feelings.

Of course it doesn't! The idea that rules alone can solve the problem of sin is the essence of legalism, and that, as we have seen, is the last thing that we could say about the Psalmist. In fact, the idea that we can solve the problem of sin by our own efforts runs contrary to the whole message of the Bible. It is certainly true that the Psalmist wants to do all that lies in his own power to *avoid* sinning against God. He is straining every fibre of his mind, his will and his emotions to resist sin. And so should we. But he knows that the final answer to his sin lies outside himself.

In the Introduction I said that Psalm 119 is not primarily about the law but about God, and in particular about the Psalmist's personal and intimate relationship with God. He is not merely trying to keep the rules because rules are rules. No, in verse 11 he expresses the truth of the matter.

I have hidden your word in my heart
  that I might not sin against you.

It is his relationship with God that he does not want to be damaged by his own sin and folly. So he knows that when he does sin, the only answer must come from God's side of the relationship.

*The only hope in the face of sin lies in God.*

But can there be any hope at all for this Psalmist then? Surely this poor Old Testament believer in his Old Testament God will have to wait until the New Testament gets going before he can expect any grace and forgiveness for his sin, won't he?

What a distortion of the Old Testament and of the God of the whole Bible! Sadly this common view is sometimes based on a misunderstanding of John 1:17: 'The law was given through Moses; grace and truth came through Jesus Christ.'

People sometimes insert a 'but' between these two clauses, as if they were in contrast. But they aren't; the second adds depth to the first. If anything, we should insert, 'Yes, and . . .' between them. Also, 'grace and truth *came*' is an inadequate translation. John actually says 'became'. That is, grace and truth became embodied, visible, real and recognizable in the person of the incarnate Jesus. John does not mean that there was no grace or truth in the Old Testament!

But let's hear the Psalmist speaking for himself. Read the following verses, preferably slowly and aloud, and let them sink in. Reflect on how the Psalmist describes God's character and attitude.

Keep me from deceitful ways;
   be gracious to me through your law (v29).

May your unfailing love come to me, O LORD,
   your salvation according to your promise (v41).

May your unfailing love be my comfort,
   according to your promise to your servant (v76).

Let your compassion come to me that I may live,
   for your law is my delight (v77).

Turn to me and have mercy on me,
  as you always do to those who love your name (v132).

Ponder these words. Did you really hear them? Grace, unfailing love, compassion and mercy. Is there anything there that you, as a Christian, do not pray for and rely on when you bring your sins in confession before God? We may do our best to avoid sin, but the only answer to sin lies in God, and specifically in his grace, love, salvation, comfort, compassion, mercy and salvation. And this is precisely the character of the God whom the Psalmist, with other Old Testament saints and believers, knew and loved.

How did he know these things about the LORD, the God of Israel? The answer can be found in verse 29 above where he actually puts grace and law in the same breath: 'Be gracious to me through your law.'

● *How does the law reveal the grace and love of God?*

Remember that for the Israelites 'The Law' was the Torah: the five books of the Pentateuch, from Genesis to Deuteronomy. What parts of those books especially reveal God's grace and mercy? Can you think of any particular stories?

Perhaps, more than any, the story of God's forgiveness of Israel's rebellion at Sinai with the Golden Calf (see Exodus 32 – 34) underlies the Psalmist's appeal to God as a God of grace 'according to your law'. For it is there that God first presented his identity badge to Moses and revealed his name and his character in one magnificent declaration that rings through the Bible in many other places.

And he passed in front of Moses, proclaiming, 'The LORD,
the LORD, the compassionate and gracious God, slow to
anger, abounding in love and faithfulness, maintaining love
to thousands, and forgiving wickedness, rebellion and sin.
Yet he does not leave the guilty unpunished' (Ex. 34:6-7).

Now of course we know that ultimately we can only speak
of God's righteousness and mercy in the light of the cross.
For there God's character was fully and finally displayed –
his wrath and his mercy; his judgment and his grace; his
condemnation of sin and his love for sinners.

But Hebrews 11 tells us that the people of faith in the Old
Testament are included with us in the great community of
those whom God has redeemed through the cross of Christ.
And in my imagination, I visualize them too looking at that
great outpouring of God's self-giving love at the cross, and
saying, 'Yes, that is our God. That is what we know that he,
and only he, could do. He is the God of love, patience, grace,
mercy and forgiveness. We knew that too. And we even
gave you the vocabulary to express it. Those were our words
for God before they became yours. We told you that the
answer to the problem of human sin could only lie in the
mercy of God himself, and now he has proved his love.'

Yes, we who are blessed to live on this side of Calvary
know the full extent of God's love in history. But I think
that nothing surpasses the language the Old Testament
provides in marvelling at the forgiving grace of God. And
personally, it is usually to these great Old Testament texts
that I find myself turning when I need to come back to
God in humble repentance, to hear again the words of
inexhaustible grace. Perhaps you would like to do the
same, and spend time pondering the majesty and comfort
of these wonderful affirmations. Some of these great
words of grace would have been known to the writer of
this psalm as he joins with us in thanking God for them.

**FURTHER STUDY**

Remind yourself of the crucifixion narrative found in Matthew 27:27-56. Spend time meditating on what it meant for Jesus to die for us. Come before God, expressing your thanks and gratitude for what he has done for us.

**REFLECTION AND RESPONSE**

Select a few of the Bible references listed below, and spend time by yourself or in a group meditating on what it means to be forgiven by God and how this should affect our lives:

Psalm 25:6-11, 32:1-5, 103:8-14, 130:3-4; Isaiah 43:25, 55:6-7, 57:15-18; Ezekiel 18:21-22, 36:25-26; Micah 7:18-19.

# Personal Struggle and the Word of Lament

**Recommended reading: Psalm 119:81-88**

# Personal Struggle and the Word of Lament

## INTRODUCTION TO SECTION 4

In Hebrew the book we call 'The Psalms' is actually termed 'The Praises'. So it is somewhat ironic that the largest single category of psalms in the book consists of *laments*! It may be more surprising to us than to the Israelites, since we have reduced the word 'praise' to a rather happy-clappy effervescence of thanksgiving and good cheer. But praise for the Israelites meant more than that. To praise God meant to acknowledge God's reality and involvement in the whole of life – whatever the circumstances. So, even when life was exceedingly tough they would turn to God and lay everything before him, sometimes in protest or lament. This was a form of praise for it was an appeal to the God they knew, loved and trusted, in spite of all temptations to the contrary.

The psalms of lament have some common features that are easily discernible. They tend to go something like this:

- *God, I'm hurting*
- *God, everybody else is attacking and laughing at me*
- *God, you're not doing much to help right now*
- *God, I still trust you, but how long will this go on, please?*

There are many psalms with these elements, but a quick look at Psalms 35, 43 and 70 will illustrate the pattern.

Psalm 119 is not strictly a psalm of lament, since it has many other elements woven into it, as we are seeing. But there is a lot of lament in it. Clearly whoever wrote this poem was having a tough time and was struggling with a lot in his life – things that caused pain, anxiety, fear and confusion. Early on in the psalm he tells us that he feels like an alien on the earth (v19), and in the very last verse he still feels like a lost sheep (v176). So this is a person in a far from happy and secure state of mind. The next three chapters will observe:

- *His dire experiences.* The Psalmist, apparently young and inexperienced, suffers contempt, slander and even conspiracy.
- *His deep reactions.* No armchair critic, he is deeply affected by the wickedness he sees in society, and pays a heavy internal emotional cost.
- *His double response.* He sees no discrepancy between crying out to God for help and at the same time gritting his teeth with determination to carry on.

# CHAPTER 8

# When life gets tough

*Aim: To face up to some of the struggles and pressures that believers face*

**FOCUS ON THE THEME**
How do you react when the going gets tough?

- Complain
- Hide under the duvet
- Phone a friend
- Pray

Changing how we respond and putting our trust in God is sometimes not easy when faced with opposition and abuse, as the Psalmist found out.

The first clue we get that all is not sunny in the garden of this Psalmist's life is when he tells us in verse 19 that he feels like 'a stranger on earth'. Something in his circumstances is making him feel out of place. Actually, as we shall see in a moment, that is putting it mildly. But this is where he starts.

Certain verses in the psalm suggest that the Psalmist may have been a young person, perhaps feeling inexperienced and vulnerable. The question of verse 9, 'How can a young man keep his way pure?' may be autobiographical – that is, he is asking the question for his own benefit. Also, in verses 99 and 100, he speaks about his teachers and elders. There are clues also that he may be involved in public or political leadership, since he seems to move in the company of rulers and kings (see vv23 and 46). So perhaps here we have someone who, though relatively young, finds himself thrust into the public arena, called on to act in a cynical world in which he feels somewhat out of his depth. He is anxious, struggling to sustain his own integrity in the face of much opposition, unsure of his own ability, but eager to sustain his confidence in God and in God's word as the foundation of his life and work.

Does that sound familiar? It may well be true of yourself, or of others known to you who are Christians in the rough and tumble world of secular (and especially civic or political) life.

There are two elements to the Psalmist's troubles that we shall consider in this chapter: the pain of scorn and contempt and the pain of slander and conspiracy.

## 1. THE PAIN OF SCORN AND CONTEMPT

*Read verses 22, 42 and 141 below.*

Remove from me scorn and contempt,
  for I keep your statutes (v22).

Then I will answer the one who taunts me,
  for I trust in your word (v42).

Though I am lowly and despised,
  I do not forget your precepts (v141).

● *Despite being scorned, taunted and despised, the Psalmist insists on obeying God's commands and trusting his word. What does this tell us about his character?*

To be laughed at or held in contempt is deeply painful and destructive. And yet it is tragically common. And it starts so young. We wince at the suffering of children who are subjected to merciless bullying – physical, verbal or social – at school. Some never even recover as adults from the continuing diminishing comments they received from their parents, often in unfair comparison to siblings. Others suffer unremitting mockery at work, or vicious racist or sexist humour and worse.

## 2. THE PAIN OF SLANDER AND CONSPIRACY

It gets worse. This person is not just getting laughed at; he is apparently in serious danger, at least some of the time. And this is an even longer catalogue. As you read this depressing list of his experiences, discuss and summarize what he is going through. As usual, it is helpful to read a few verses either side of the quoted verse to get the context.

Though rulers sit together and slander me,
  your servant will meditate on your decrees (v23).

Though the arrogant have smeared me with lies,
  I keep your precepts with all my heart (v69).

May the arrogant be put to shame for wronging me
  without cause;
  but I will meditate on your precepts (v78).

How long must your servant wait?
  When will you punish my persecutors?

The arrogant dig pitfalls for me,
  contrary to your law.

All your commands are trustworthy;
    help me, for men persecute me without cause (vv84-86).

The wicked are waiting to destroy me,
    but I will ponder your statutes (v95).

The wicked have set a snare for me,
    but I have not strayed from your precepts (v110).

I have done what is righteous and just;
    do not leave me to my oppressors (v121).

Redeem me from the oppression of men,
    that I may obey your precepts (v134).

Many are the foes who persecute me,
    but I have not turned from your statutes (v157).

Rulers persecute me without cause,
    but my heart trembles at your word (v161).

Now this could be dismissed as a case of acute paranoia. But if not, if this guy is telling us the truth about what he is going through, then he is having a tough time of the highest order. As we noted, he may well be in some position of public and political leadership, where back-stabbing conspiracy, entrapment, unjust accusation and character assassination by whispering lies are all familiar occupational hazards.

Daniel knew such a world. He was a civil servant in high government office. There were those who trusted him and there were those who hated him. And the hatred *from his peers and juniors* was a mixture of racist and religious prejudice and professional jealousy. Unfortunately, his enemies could find no corruption or accusation of negligence or laziness that had any chance of sticking, so they engineered his downfall, not through his weakness, but through his strongest distinguishing characteristic – his faith and prayer-life.

Briefly remind yourself of the story of Daniel 6. Note especially verses 3-5.

- *In what ways does Daniel's experience reflect Psalm 119? In what ways do both texts speak into your own experience?*
- *How should we pray for Christians in leadership roles or those with high responsibility? How can we encourage them?*

We have been thinking about public or political leadership, but of course any leadership role exposes you to the jealousies, misinterpretation and attacks of others. And Christian leadership is no exception. In fact it can sometimes be even worse – tragic, but true.

- *Pastors and ministers can struggle with opposition and criticism (like Moses); trying to lead those who refuse to be led; trying to share a vision with those who are wilfully blind.*
- *Cross-cultural missionaries can endure physical hardship. Often living in the midst of religious oppression, they may experience actual danger or the suffering misinterpretation of their motives.*

But apart from those in positions of leadership, the words of the Psalmist ring true in many other situations, some of which are listed below. Reflect on these and discuss any other examples that you can think of.

- *Christians in a non-Christian family may have to endure much misunderstanding and abuse.*

- *Christians in hostile workplaces may face discrimination. A stand for honesty or truth-telling can be seriously unpopular. In countries where another religion dominates society, being a Christian may rule out any chances of promotion and guarantee a life of constant harassment or worse.*

- *Christian young people who choose to live their lives in accordance with biblical standards of behaviour, especially in sexual ethics, encounter incomprehension at best and scorn and being viciously pilloried at worst.*

Finally, there are many of us who, while we may not suffer abuse in any way comparable to what the Psalmist describes, can easily translate these words of mockery, taunting, oppression, smearing and lies, into the spiritual reality of satanic assault. We know only too well the inner voices of attack that stir up within us:

- *Fear.* Fear can be debilitating: 'You'll never succeed', 'You'll never get better.'

- *Self-accusation.* We do a very effective job in smearing ourselves with lies, when we refuse to believe the truth that God says of us, and go on giving credence to all kinds of negative assertions.

- *Guilt.* Satan exploits objective guilt for real sins and our guilty feelings – whether fanciful or justified. So even after we have taken them to the cross, confessed them and been forgiven, the old accuser persecutes us with guilt we no longer bear.

- *Self-pity and bitterness.* It is a short step from real and actual suffering of wrong, to wallowing in a perpetual sludge of *feeling* wronged and victimized. It is a kind of inverse pride, and since it is almost impervious to repentance, Satan loves it, stokes and kindles it within us.

You may recognize some of these 'enemies'. And you may be able to name a few more. But whatever your experience in these things, here is someone who has walked where you walk, sat where you sit, struggled and wept and protested as you may have done.

And there are others like him in the Bible. Jeremiah and Job both suffered so much that they wished they had never been born.

---

**FURTHER STUDY**

Read Jeremiah 15:10, 15-18; 20:7-18; Job 3.

- In what ways does the fact that God allows such laments and protests as these to be part of the Bible bring us encouragement in tough times?

- How can we make more use of such texts, as individuals and as a church? In what contexts?

**REFLECTION AND RESPONSE**

We shouldn't end this chapter without reference to Jesus. Read 1 Peter 2:20-23. Reflect on how the example of Jesus impacts on all you have discussed in this chapter and how this relates to the way the Psalmist prays about his problems.

# CHAPTER 9

# How does it feel?

*Aim: To be honest about our emotional responses to evil*

**FOCUS ON THE THEME**
How are you feeling? You could be tired, sad, happy, angry, worried or anxious about a number of things. Why are you feeling like this? Grab a copy of this week's newspaper. How do you react to what you read? Do you have the same intensity of feeling about national and international issues as you do about more personal matters?

One thing about this Psalmist is that you always know exactly how he feels. He doesn't hesitate to express his thoughts and emotions in graphic language. Having looked at the Psalmist's experience of opposition and suffering, we turn now to his soul. What is all this doing to him emotionally? We will notice two things: first, the Psalmist's reaction to the evil outside; and second his response to the pain inside.

The aim of this study is to be as honest with ourselves as this Psalmist was with his readers. That in itself is not easy, but it is the first step towards receiving the help we need from God and one another.

## 1. THE EVIL OUTSIDE

So much of what goes on in the world is nasty, brutish and downright evil. How do we react? What thoughts fill our minds as we read our newspapers or watch the TV news, and find our senses assaulted with yet another spectacle of genocide or brutality, or one more sickening tale of sexual abuse of children, or the astonishing hypocrisy of politicians caught in a web of deceit?

Our Psalmist is no passive observer. He is not a cynical commentator, gleefully exposing the wickedness of others with a callous shrug or a knowing wink. His is not the spurious self-righteousness of the gutter press that shrieks with apoplectic headlines against public figures caught in sexual scandal, while simultaneously feeding salacious fantasies on the inside pages.

On the contrary, he cares so deeply about God and God's law that he is terribly distressed at the blatant evil and corruption he sees around him. It is almost too painful to bear.

● *Read through the verses below and reflect on the Psalmist's reactions to external wickedness. Discuss the different emotions displayed. In each case, what is the reason he feels such things?*

Indignation grips me because of the wicked,
  who have forsaken your law (v53).

I hate double-minded men,
  but I love your law (v113).

Away from me, you evildoers,
  that I may keep the commands of my God! (v115).

Streams of tears flow from my eyes,
  for your law is not obeyed (v136).

My zeal wears me out,
  for my enemies ignore your word (v139).

I look on the faithless with loathing,
  for they do not obey your word (v158).

These are far from pleasant emotions. In fact, in many circumstances some of these would be sinful. Yet, as reactions against sin and wickedness, which is what they are in this context, they actually reflect something of God's own reaction to evil. We already touched on this point in our study on Personal Sin and the Word of Grace.

This Psalmist, through his saturation in the Scriptures, knows how God feels about sin and indeed how God will eventually act against those who are persistently, unrepentantly wicked.

- *God will rebuke them (v21)*
- *God will reject them (v118)*
- *God will discard them (v119)*

And it is high time he did so, in the Psalmist's opinion (v126)!

Now of course, the Bible has a great deal more to say about God's love for sinners and God's longing for their repentance, forgiveness and restoration. As a forgiven sinner himself, this Psalmist would not deny that; on the contrary, he relies upon it. But the Bible strongly asserts that ingrained, persistent human wickedness stirs the anger of God and ultimately brings his judgment.

This raises questions about our own reaction to sin and wickedness in the world around us.

- *Does the language of this psalm reflect the emotions that we should have as Christians in response to evil, or do you*

*reject such language as inappropriate? On what grounds did
you answer either way?*

● *What makes you angry as you listen to the news or read the
newspapers? For example it could be the abuse of power,
injustice, cruelty, the state of the health service or the
government.*

● *Analyse your response. Could it be that your own selfish
interests are being threatened? Is your response coloured by
your political preferences and loyalties, or by social
prejudices? Or is your anger tested by clear biblical values?*

What about *the target* of our anger, even when we sincerely
believe that our anger is directed against sin? It is easy to
become selective and one-sided on some issues, to
overheat on some moral issues, and overlook others.

Tony Campolo is said to have once announced in a large
public gathering that during the course of his talk thousands
of the poorest people in the world would die of hunger, 'and
most of you don't give a \*\*\*\*!' he exclaimed. There was a
shocked silence; some people got up and walked out. 'The
real shame,' he went on, 'is that some of you are more
morally offended by one bad word than by world poverty
and hunger.' And he was right, of course. Ezekiel was
prepared to use foul language to shock his audience with
the far worse moral evil of their own social and private lives.

The question we have to ask is, what makes God most
angry? And where can we find an answer to that question?
From the Scriptures of course – as did the Psalmist. Did
you notice that the primary reason why he reacts as he
does is because people are not obeying God's word? So
what kind of wickedness does the Bible emphasize?

Well, we might answer, an awful lot of it! But there are
some clues as to what God hates most. For example, there
is the word 'abomination'. In Hebrew the word means

something that fills God with disgust and revulsion, something he simply cannot stomach. If you do a word search on abomination you will find that it covers a surprising list of things. While it includes various forms of sexual perversion and immorality, it also includes dishonest scales (Prov. 11:1; 20:10,23) – that is, cheating in trade and business. And if we still feel well out of range of the word's moral firing-power, here are some other things that stink in God's nostrils as abominations.

- *False witness (Jer. 7:9; Ezek. 22:9; Prov. 6:19)*
- *Lying in general (Prov. 6:16-17; 12:22; 26:25-28)*
- *Neglect of the poor and needy (Ezek. 16:47-52; 18:7; 22:7)*
- *Contempt for parents (Ezek. 22:7)*
- *Arrogance (Prov. 6:16-19)*
- *Hypocritical worship (Isa. 1:13; Prov. 21:27; 28:9)*

Or we might think of the things that the Bible places under God's curse. Yes, these include idolatry, incest, sexual immorality and murder. But the list also includes abusing the disabled, bribery, and 'the man who withholds justice from the alien, the fatherless and the widow' (Deut. 27:19).

Turn to Romans 1:18-32 where we find Paul's catalogue of endemic human sin. What did you notice about the list mentioned? Again, we find reference to sexual immorality, murder and depravity. But what other sins are listed? What does this passage teach us about God's standard for living?

My point is that we need to educate our anger. That is, we need to have an awareness of *all* that the Bible condemns, and be more consistent and more biblically orientated in the things that stir our emotions and draw our protests.

As evangelical Christians we tend to have our moral consciences very sensitively tuned to sexual problems and generate a huge quantity of moral (and ecclesiastical) energy in that direction. There is no doubt that the Bible speaks clearly on sexual ethics and we need to stand for biblical truth in that area. However, it grieves me that nothing like the same moral energy or anger tends to be directed towards social and economic wickedness – perhaps because it is less easy to be sure of the cleanness of our own hands. How disturbed are we, how angry do we find ourselves when we hear of the plight of refugees, asylum seekers, the homeless, the landless, the family-less, the poor and needy, the victims of oppression, injustice and debt? And yet the anger of God against such things is revealed with devastating clarity throughout the Bible, and with much more textual weight than all it has to say on sexual ethics.

● *How is your church involved in supporting particular moral campaigns in society, or taking a stand on certain ethical issues within the church itself? What should our attitudes be towards such things?*

  *Discuss and evaluate these in relation to the Bible's 'ethical priority index'.*

## 2. THE PAIN INSIDE

What was all this struggle and distress doing to the Psalmist? We have seen his emotions in relation to external wickedness. But he was also suffering opposition, mockery, slander, false accusation, and possibly even physical threat. So how did he cope with it? What did it all feel like?

● *Once again, we can make a chain of places where he pours out his feelings. Read the verses below and reflect on how the Psalmist feels in each case.*

I am laid low in the dust;
  preserve my life according to your word (v25).

My soul is weary with sorrow;
  strengthen me according to your word (v28).

My comfort in my suffering is this:
  Your promise preserves my life (v50).

My soul faints with longing for your salvation,
  but I have put my hope in your word.
My eyes fail, looking for your promise;
  I say, 'When will you comfort me?'
Though I am a wineskin in the smoke,
  I do not forget your decrees (vv81-83).

If your law had not been my delight,
  I would have perished in my affliction (v92).

I have suffered much;
  preserve my life, O LORD, according to your word (v107).

My zeal wears me out,
  for my enemies ignore your words (v139).

What a list of inner pain and struggle! If this person had lived today, he would have been recommended for counselling and a strong dose of pastoral care. The symptoms he describes could refer to depression, dryness, fainting with exhaustion, extreme weakness and general suffering. It is likely that in your study group there will be some who can identify with some of these. The comfort is that the Bible includes such expressions of pain, allows them to be voiced in the presence of God, and points us in the direction of healing – namely to God himself, his word, his promise and his life-giving strength.

But it is worth noting one more thing as we finish. These words of suffering, struggle, weakness and depression come from the lips of one who is a faithful believer. Here is somebody who is sincerely trusting God and doing his absolute utmost to live in obedience to God. And yet his testimony is not one of abundant blessings, spectacular outpourings of wealth, or instant healing of all his pains.

---

**REFLECTION AND RESPONSE**

This psalm exposes what a fraudulent travesty and deception the so-called 'prosperity gospel' is. What do you understand by this phrase? Why is it such an attractive teaching? Discuss within your group the dangers of such teaching.[7]

You may find the following helpful to stimulate group discussion

- 'Prosperity' teaching is a spiritual perversion of the Bible. It plays upon our endemic selfishness and greed, and causes immense pastoral damage.

- While the Bible certainly gives examples of people whom God signally blessed with material abundance, it is equally rich in examples of those who suffered greatly, not because of a lack of faith but because of their resolute faith and obedience to God.

- The Bible is full of warnings that it is possible to be exceedingly wealthy, not as a result of God's blessing but from the profits of oppression and wickedness.

**FURTHER STUDY**

Read 2 Corinthians 10:17-18, 21b-30. Reflect on what Paul suffered for the gospel. How did he respond and what lessons can you draw from this for your own Christian life?

# CHAPTER 10

# Pressing on

*Aim: To recommit ourselves to the balance of trust and perseverance*

**FOCUS ON THE THEME**
Read 2 Corinthians 4:7-18. Spend a few minutes meditating on Paul's words before beginning this study.

In our last two studies we have tried to enter into the circumstances that have made the Psalmist's life so tough, and we have listened to the way he voices his emotions in response to the evil in the world outside and the pain inside his own heart.

But what did he actually do about all this? The answer is twofold. On the one hand, he cries out desperately to God for help; on the other, he grits his teeth and gets on with the game. He pleads upwards and he presses onwards.

## 1. HE CRIES OUT TO GOD

*Read verses 81-88.* It is the cry of endurance, the cry of a desperate, seemingly endless, waiting for God. It is one long drawn out expansion of its central question, 'How long must your servant wait?' (v84). 'I waited patiently for the LORD', says Psalm 40 – and sometimes not so patiently. 'Lord, when will you hear? When will you answer? When will you do something?' Many of us know that place and those prayers all too well.

*Read verses 145-148.*

> I call with all my heart; answer me, O LORD,
>   and I will obey your decrees.
> I call out to you; save me
>   and I will keep your statutes.
> I rise before dawn and cry for help;
>   I have put my hope in your word.
> My eyes stay open through the watches of the night,
>   that I may meditate on your promises.

Sleepless nights and early mornings accompany a deep longing for God to hear him. What reason does he have to persist in his confident hope that God will eventually answer and act? Three things stand out: because God is near, God is a shelter and God is the God of the exodus.

### 1. Because God is as near as his troubles are

Or rather, God is even nearer than his troubles. There is a wonderful double play on words in verses 150-151.

> Those who devise wicked schemes are near,
>   but they are far from your law.
> Yet you are near, O LORD,
>   and all your commands are true.

● *There is a parallelism here. What is the Psalmist saying?*

The paradox is that the wicked who are causing such trouble seem very near to the Psalmist, but they are far from God; whereas God, who seems to be far away from the Psalmist (vv145-146), is actually near to him.

The nearness of God is a great biblical promise. It is worth remembering when our troubles are bearing down on us. God is nearer than any threat.

I remember a moment in an England football match when an attacker was bearing down on goalkeeper David Seaman – one on one, and a goal seemed certain, when suddenly out of nowhere (off camera) Sol Campbell appeared and robbed the attacker of the ball. At the moment of greatest danger, the unseen defender was even nearer than the striker.

● *Can you list any other Bible texts about the nearness of God? Think about which Bible stories illustrate God's nearness at times of great trouble or danger.*

### 2. Because God is a great place to hide

> You are my refuge and my shield;
>   I have put my hope in your word (v114).

In a storm, you need a shelter. If you are being chased, you need a hiding place. In a bombing raid, you need a bunker. When you were a child you hid under the blankets, or ran to your mother's arms. This metaphor of God as a place to hide is a favourite among the Psalmists. We have a deep need to be safe and secure, and God is the ultimate provider of that. There are times when we feel so exposed and under attack that running 'into God' as the place of shelter and protection is enormously reassuring.

> The name of the LORD is a strong tower.
>   The righteous run to it, and are safe (Prov. 18:10).

When I was Principal at All Nations Christian College, there were often times when as a community we were conscious of spiritual attack by the forces of the evil one. As a college dedicated to training people for cross-cultural mission that would advance the kingdom of God, this was not at all unexpected. That did not make it any less unpleasant and sometimes almost overwhelming. I remember one occasion when my senior staff team felt there was a particular focus of satanic attack upon myself as Principal. We spent time in urgent prayer together. And one of my staff prayed a prayer I cannot forget and often reclaim. 'Lord,' she prayed, 'please hide Chris under your wings so that the devil won't even know where to find him.' I felt safe after that!

### 3. Because God is the God of the exodus

> Look upon my suffering and deliver me;
>   for I have not forgotten your law.
> Defend my cause and redeem me;
>   preserve my life according to your promise.
> Salvation is far from the wicked,
>   for they do not seek out your decrees.
> Your compassion is great O LORD;
>   preserve my life according to your laws (vv153-156).

● *Compare the language of the psalm with the narrative of the exodus as recorded in Exodus 2 – 6. Notice in particular Exodus 2:23-25; 3:7-9; 6:2-8.*

All that the Psalmist is appealing to, he already knows about God from the story of the exodus. He is asking God to do for him what he originally did for his ancestors, and for the same reasons.

Israel worshipped the God who was not blind. No matter how much the wicked seemed to prosper and the righteous seemed to suffer interminably, it would not always stay that way. God sees and knows. God cares and acts. God will ultimately defend and redeem his people – including his faithful, praying believer.

Where did the Psalmist get all this understanding of God from? He has been telling us again and again – from the Torah. The Psalmist himself had not been personally present, of course, at the exodus. But he knew the story and the story sustained his faith and hope. This is our God, he reminded himself. This is what he promised and accomplished. This is my God too, he goes on, so I will call out to him in the confidence of being heard. He will save and defend me.

Cry out to God in your troubles, by all means. But make sure you know the God you are crying out to. Make sure it is this God, the biblical God; the God you know through deep immersion in his word.

## 2. HE DETERMINES TO PRESS ON

Psalm 119 resonates with the sound of gritting teeth. The Psalmist is determined that, no matter what happens, however great the opposition, and whatever the cost, he will go on obeying, trusting, serving and loving God. He will not give up. He is exercising his will again. He affirms his stubborn determination to see it through even in the toughest times.

Is this a contradiction? Is it wrong to ask God for help and yet talk about your own efforts and determination? Is it confusing grace and works if we say, 'God, you've got to help me, and I cry out to you,' and then say 'God, I'm determined to keep going, to persevere and struggle through this tough patch'? Hardly, for both are fully expressed by this one psalm without any sense of conflict between the one and the other.

Look at the contrasts in verses 81 and 83. The first half of each verse is the longing and exhaustion and cry to God, but the second half is the personal determination: 'I have put my hope in your word'; 'I do not forget your decrees.' Hope and obedience are to be worked at. God doesn't do them for us; we determine to exercise them ourselves. So the Psalmist says he will press on. In fact, he will do so with enthusiasm. Look at verses 28 and 32. In verse 28 we hear the cry.

> My soul is weary with sorrow;
>> strengthen me according to your word.

But in verse 32 he gathers that strength and says

> I will run in the path of your commands,
>> for you have set my heart free.

So here is somebody who is not just going to crawl doggedly forward in the dust. He's going to pick himself up and run in the path of obedience and the joy of spiritual freedom.

He also reflects on the fact that some of the struggles that God has allowed him to go through have had a positive effect. *Read verses 67, 71 and 75.*

> Before I was afflicted I went astray,
>> but now I obey your word (v67).

> It was good for me to be afflicted
>> so that I might learn your decrees (v71).

> I know, O LORD, that your laws are righteous,
>> and in faithfulness you have afflicted me (v75).

- *What benefit has affliction brought to him?*
- *Does this mean that the affliction itself was good?*

When God allows affliction, he does not stop being faithful – to us or to himself. This is never an easy lesson to learn. No affliction ever seems a good thing at the time. But just as the irritation of the grain of sand produces the pearl, so the struggles God allows us to go through can produce good fruit – provided we choose to persevere in them with God.

- *How does what the New Testament says about affliction, struggle and suffering reflect the faith and determination of Psalm 119? Read and discuss the following passages, noticing the same balance of reliance on God along with persevering patience and effort. 2 Corinthians 1:3-11; 11:23-30; 12:7-10 Hebrews 12:1-12*

So we need, then, to hold on to this balance between full confidence in God, on the one hand, and courageous personal perseverance, on the other. There are plenty of biblical examples of both for our instruction.

There are times when we cry

> Lord, I call out to you again. Lord, I long for you to act. I am desperate for you to sort out this problem, or to put right this mess. Lord I need you urgently and I know that only you can deal with an issue as big as this one. You are my only hope.

And yet at the same time we say to him

> But Lord, I am still here waiting in patience. And I want you to know that no matter what you do, and no matter what you don't do, I'll still be here. You're stuck with me. I'm not

going anywhere else. I am your servant; I love you; I trust you. And I'm going to battle on serving you no matter what other people, or Satan, or even you, throw at me. I'm in this for the long haul, for a long obedience in one direction only. For frankly I don't know where else I would go, or what else I would do – if I ever gave up on this determination to love and to serve you, the only living God.

This is the voice that we hear from our Psalmist. It is also the voice that we hear in the Garden of Gethsemane. There we see the agonizing struggle going on in the humanity of the Son of God himself. He cries out to God in desperate fear of what the next few hours would bring him, 'Lord, if it be possible, take this cup from me.' But immediately he recovers the habit of his whole lifetime and bends his own will to his Father's: 'Nevertheless, not my will, but yours be done.' And then in that determination to do what he had come to do, he got up from his knees and walked forward to his arrest, trial, flogging and crucifixion. No one shows us more clearly what utter dependence on God means than Jesus. And no one shows us more clearly either utter determination to press on and do God's will, against all the forces of evil ranged against him.

**FURTHER STUDY**

Turn to the examples of Daniel and Job (Daniel 3 and Job 1:6-22, 12-14). How do they respond in affliction?

Read Nehemiah 2:1-5 (you might want to read Nehemiah 1 to get the context). How does he exemplify the double strategy the Psalmist exemplifies in this psalm? What can this teach us about our own attitude towards struggles and hardships?

**REFLECTION AND RESPONSE**

As a group, spend time exercising both parts of this double response on behalf of each other. Put each other's needs before God, crying to him to hear and answer as you put your hope and trust in him. Then encourage one another in the daily task of pressing on in faith and obedience.

Read Psalm 40 aloud together and make it your own confession.

# Personal Renewal and the Word of Life

**Recommended reading: Psalm 119:153-160**

# Personal Renewal and the Word of Life

## INTRODUCTION TO SECTION 5

*'I shouldn't be here.'* These are the words spoken directly to the camera by a number of ordinary people in succession, as they are enjoying a game of tennis, or a family meal. It is a TV advertisement being screened frequently in the UK as I write – an advertisement asking people to give generously to Cancer Research UK. The point they are making is that, without the life-saving treatment they had received, they would be dead by now. They shouldn't be here, but they are, because the treatment has given them a new and unexpected lease of life. The moving appeal is that viewers should give the gift of life to others through supporting research.

Life. We cling to it, and at times we feel desperately in need of having our lives refreshed and renewed, protected or prolonged. That is certainly the mood of the Psalmist.

I was struck, when I started really reading this psalm in depth, how frequently this theme comes. As we saw, there are 22 sections in the psalm. In 11 of these, and no less than 14 times the Psalmist prays, 'Renew my life', or in the various ways it is translated, 'restore my life, give me life, preserve my life, let me live.' In the majority of cases, these are different ways of rendering a single dramatic exclamation in Hebrew: *'Hayyeni!'* Literally it means, 'Cause me to live! Make me live! "Life" me!' It is a prayer that grows more intense and repeated towards the end of the psalm, and indeed is almost his final prayer, in the last verse but one.

● *Pause and read the following verses. Read them aloud if possible, one after the other, to feel their combined effect and the strength of feeling that goes into this appeal.*

Do good to your servant, and I will live;
 I will obey your word (v17).

I am laid low in the dust;
 preserve my life according to your word (v25).

Turn my eyes away from worthless things;
 preserve my life according to your word (v37).

How I long for your precepts!
 Preserve my life in your righteousness (v40).

My comfort in my suffering is this:
 Your promise preserves my life (v50).

Let your compassion come to me that I may live,
 for your law is my delight (v77).

I have suffered much;
 preserve my life, O LORD, according to your word (v107).

Sustain me according to your promise, and I shall live;
 do not let my hopes be dashed (v116).

Your statutes are for ever right;
 give me understanding that I may live (v144).

Hear my voice in accordance with your love;
 preserve my life, O LORD, according to your laws (v149).

Defend my cause and redeem me;
   preserve my life according to your promise (v154).

Your compassion is great, O LORD;
   preserve my life according to your laws (v156).

See how I love your precepts;
   preserve my life, O LORD, according to your love (v159).

Let me live that I may praise you,
   and may your laws sustain me (v175).

Did you notice, first, how some situation of threat or difficulty is often referred to – something that is anti-life? In the Psalmist's experience, depression, exhaustion, temptation, hostility and suffering, all make him 'die a little.' So in chapter 11 we will think about those *threats to life*.

Then, secondly, notice that when the Psalmist asks God to renew his life, he often makes his appeal on the basis of some fact about God – either God's character (his righteousness, or compassion, or love), or God's word (his law and his promises). We shall think about those *sources of life* in chapter 12.

And thirdly, it is worth noticing that sometimes the Psalmist 'encourages' God to renew his life with a few suggestions as to what will happen if he does! For the Psalmist there would be renewed strength, comfort and hope, of course. But for God there would be renewed obedience and amplified praise coming from the renewed life of his servant. This will form our concluding reflection in this amazing Psalmist's company.

# CHAPTER 11

# Threats to life

*Aim: To identify and recognize things that may be more life-threatening than we think*

> **FOCUS ON THE THEME**
> Read 2 Corinthians 4:11-12. What are some of the ways in which we can see 'death at work in us' and in the world around us? How are we to respond to this dying and decaying world?

Many things in life are deadly. That is, they are anti-life; they spoil life; they suck the life out of you. Of course, the great original anti-life is sin – as we have known since the Garden of Eden. 'On the day you eat of it, you will die . . . Dust you are and to dust you will return.' And as Paul also said, through sin death entered human life and history. So sin is the ultimate source of death. But that does not mean that everything that threatens our enjoyment of life is a result of our own sin. Sometimes it is just the fact that we live in a fallen, sinful, death-ridden world. Although we are alive in this world, we live in the midst of death, threatened and invaded by it, and by its precursors – namely the things that rob us of life in the abundance that God intended for us.

In chapter 8 we looked at some of the struggles the Psalmist is going through. But now we notice how he singles out several things that particularly threaten the life he believes he should have from God. These are things that may not be literally fatal, but nevertheless they are deadening and debilitating. They spoil that enjoyment of life that God wants for us. From the list of verses you read in the Introduction to Section 5, I think we can discern three particular things that the Psalmist sees as threats to life in this sense – three contexts in which he asks God, by contrast, to preserve or renew his life. These are *depression*, *selfishness* and *hostility*.

## 1. THE THREAT OF DEPRESSION AND EXHAUSTION

Read verses 25 and 28. They speak of being laid low in the dust, of being utterly exhausted and worn out. Dust in itself, of course, is an echo of the dust of death in Genesis 3:19. Likewise, the teacher in Ecclesiastes ends his poetic meditation on death with the dust to which we all return (Ecc. 12:7). But here in Psalm 119 is someone who feels he is eating the dust already. Life is dried and shrivelled. I think the language of depression is not inappropriate for what is being described here.

Depression can, of course, be a relatively mild thing, when life is on the down-side for a while; you may feel miserable generally or about something more specific. But the Psalmist is probably talking about more than feeling depressed for a few days. We know that in fact *being* depressed can be a terrible, frightening experience. It may be caused by prolonged stress, emotional pressures, unresolved traumas and broken relationships, bereavement, and many other sometimes inexplicable factors – and it can also have physiological dimensions. It can certainly constitute a serious clinical illness. Some of us may have been there, and many of us will have family members or friends who suffer from serious depression, and we know something of how brutal it can be.

One of the things I have frequently heard from those I know who suffer from periodic bouts of depression is exactly what this Psalmist seems to say. Life doesn't seem worth living any more. All the point has gone out of it. There is no joy or hope in anything – even in the simplest of pleasures that are part of the fabric of everyday life. Favourite food loses its flavour. Everything seems under a cloud of futility. Depression, in that sense, is life-destroying. You don't have to be physically dead to feel as if you might as well be. Death has impinged on life.

And believers are not at all immune to it. They can be among the godliest, most committed people I know, filled with the Spirit of God, living lives of Christlikeness and service to God – but sometimes, like this Psalmist, 'laid low in the dust.' It's not because they haven't got faith, or that they don't pray enough, any more than you could say this about our Psalmist.

I have been writing this chapter while taking Bible ministry with a group of mission personnel working in a tough part of Africa. During the week one woman shared with me in some depth her struggles. Her commitment to serving in Chad for 17 years has taken its toll on her health, with some bouts of chronic fatigue. She loves the Lord, she loves his word; she loves the work she does. The problem is there is too much of it – she gets overloaded with labours and the expectations of others. Exhaustion breeds dusty dryness of spirit, depressed and guilty feelings, and fear of relapse into debilitating illness. She needed – and we prayed together – that God should renew and restore her life. The prayer of this Psalmist is exactly her longing.

● *It could be that you feel you need to talk to someone about the issues that have been raised here. This could be difficult to do, but discussing this with a close friend or Christian counsellor could help.*

● *Alternatively, read Psalm 102:1-11 together and try to enter into the life-sucking experience of the Psalmist. This psalm is described in its heading as 'A prayer of an afflicted man. When he is faint and pours out his lament before the LORD.' Try to capture the Psalmist's feelings by writing out this passage in your own paraphrase.*

Now we are not told whether this person goes through such torment because of sickness, or sin, or exhaustion, or opposition – but whatever it is, did you notice the symptoms? Loss of any sense of time and purpose; inner pain; loss of appetite; loss of weight; loss of friends; loss of sleep . . .

It is out of such depths that the cry comes, *'Lord, give me back my life!'*

## 2. THE THREAT OF SELFISH OBSESSION WITH WORTHLESS THINGS

This is the second life-threatening, death-injecting thing that the Psalmist brings to God asking for deliverance. It comes out in verses 36-37 in which the cry for life is heard.

Turn my heart toward your statutes
and not toward selfish gain (v36).

Turn my eyes away from worthless things;
preserve my life according to your word (v37).

● *In what ways is 'selfish gain' contrary to God's statutes? What did Jesus say about our hearts and our treasure (Mt. 5:19-21)?*
● *In what ways are 'worthless things' the enemy of life?*

● *Is there a difference between 'turn my heart' and 'turn my eyes'? Think about this in relation to where temptation usually starts and where it usually ends.*

The Psalmist is wise enough to discern that when you focus on your own desires, obsessed by greed and covetousness and material gain, it actually delivers the opposite effect. Instead of gaining anything, you lose everything. Instead of getting a better life, you risk losing the life you had.

Jesus gives us the same warning. 'What good will it be for a man if he gains the whole world, yet forfeits his soul? Or what can a man give in exchange for his soul?' (Mt. 16:26). The Psalmist, aware at least in some measure of this danger, prays that God will keep him from becoming so obsessed with things that will waste his life – things that promise life but deliver death.

'Selfish gain' and 'worthless things', of course, cover a lot of possibilities. Certainly one of them, and one of the most dangerous, is material wealth. Once again, Jesus gave us one of his sharpest warnings about that: 'Watch out! Be on your guard against all kinds of greed; a man's life does not consist in the abundance of his possessions' (Lk. 12:15).

Then there was Jesus' encounter with the rich young man (Mt. 19:16-22) who actually asked Jesus, like this Psalmist, for his recipe for eternal life. The man wanted to be among those who would stand among the redeemed and righteous people of God on the last day, inheriting the life of the age to come, the new life of the kingdom of God that Jesus was talking about. And Jesus told him. Among other things, he put his finger on the thing in his life that was actually standing in the way of inheriting real life – the thing that was death-dealing. It was his obsession with his personal wealth and his refusal to let it go and follow

Jesus. The tragedy of that story is that, having been pointed to the way of life, the rich young man turned around and walked away sad, returning to the way of death. He would not allow Jesus to do what this Psalmist prays for – to turn his heart away from selfish gain and worthless things, in order to find renewal of life according to the word of the Lord.

● *Take stock. Are there things in your life that could be described as 'worthless things' or 'selfish gain'? Be careful to distinguish them from ordinary pleasures and relaxations that God blesses us with and invites us to enjoy.*

● *What will it mean for you to recognize the threat such things pose to God's purpose for your life?*

● *Pray, with the Psalmist, 'Lord, renew my life according to your word' – recognizing that such renewal may need to come along with repentance and some fresh resolution and exercise of the will, as we were thinking in chapter 6.*

## 3. THE THREAT OF SUFFERING AND HOSTILITY

The third life-threatening set of circumstances that we hear about when the Psalmist prays for God to preserve or renew his life is suffering, and especially (I think), suffering caused by the hostility, opposition or criticism of others.

*Read verses 50, 107 and 154.*

My comfort in my suffering is this:
 Your promise preserves my life (v50).

I have suffered much;
  preserve my life, O LORD, according to your word (v107).

Defend my cause and redeem me;
  preserve my life according to your promise (v154).

It is the third verse that gives the clue. 'Redeem me' does not mean that the Psalmist is asking for personal forgiveness for his own sin. No, he is asking for deliverance from the attacks of others. He needs rescue. He needs somebody to take his side and stand up for him. This suggests that the suffering in verses 50 and 107 lies along the same lines as we observed in chapter 8 – that is, it was being caused by the sustained hostility and opposition this person was enduring in whatever public role he was trying to fulfil. And the Psalmist cries out for God not only to comfort him, defend him and redeem him; he asks God to preserve his life. The guy is being hounded to death. This prolonged hostility is crushing the life out of him.

We've seen that it can be a deathly thing to live with the internalized pain of depression. It can also be deathly to live with the external pain of constant criticism, opposition and hostility. Of course, we know that many Christians have to live with opposition and even persecution from non-Christian family, or work colleagues, or political authorities in some countries. But within the Christian church itself, sadly, there are people who ought to know better who go around making life a misery for their pastors and leaders. And it can be soul-destroying, life-crushing and death-dealing.

You may have been there, and know something of that gloomy numbness that comes when constant criticism squeezes the life and joy out of you. If that's the case, Psalms 55 and 56 were written with you in mind. There are times when you probably long, like the Psalmist, for the wings of a dove, to be able to fly away and leave it all behind (Ps. 55:6-8). And there are other times when you hold on grimly to the great affirmation of Psalm 56:9b-11.

By this I will know that God is for me.
In God, whose word I praise,
  in the LORD, whose word I praise –
in God I trust; I will not be afraid.
  What can man do to me?

Or it could be that you are among those who deal out the criticism relentlessly. Can I urge you to be cautious? No matter how justified you and your friends may feel your complaints and opposition to be, be careful. Maybe you do it out of what you think are the best of motives. But make sure you do it (if you have to) also as before the Lord, and with his spirit of grace and compassion. If you have to 'speak the truth in love' (another sadly abused verse, unfortunately), make sure it is constructive, not destructive; life-giving, not life-sapping. Christian leaders can be criticized to death. Don't be among the assassins.

---

### FURTHER STUDY
Do you have a favourite Bible passage to turn to in trouble and conflict? There are some wonderful words of encouragement in the Bible. Turn to Isaiah 55:6-13 and let this inspire words of praise and thankfulness to our God, despite the present circumstances or difficulties you may be in.

### REFLECTION AND RESPONSE
The Psalmist prays repeatedly for renewal of life. He recognizes that we live in a world where our lives are invaded constantly by things

that reek of death – emotionally, spiritually, psychologically, even when they are not a threat to our physical lives. Like the Psalmist, we need to identify such things, name them and shame them, and claim the power of the life-giving God over them.

What then could be eating away at your life? It could be unconfessed sin (e.g. see Ps. 32). Or it could be stubbornness, pride, self-pity. It could be disobedience, or an ungodly relationship.

Whatever it is, recognize the life-threatening nature of it, and make the Psalmist's prayer your own: 'Lord, renew my life, restore my life, give my life back and let me live it fully for you.'

CHAPTER 12

# Sources of life

*Aim: To remind ourselves of the true meaning and source of renewal*

**FOCUS ON THE THEME**
Read Deuteronomy 30:19-20 before you start this study (this passage may well have been in the Psalmist's mind). What does it mean in your own daily life (or in the experience of members of the group), to 'Choose life', and to acknowledge that 'the Lord is your life'?

'I'm Martin, I'm here, and I'm alive,' he said, at the start of a sharing time during the conference in Africa that I mentioned in the last chapter. Martin's testimony was that, though it was obvious he was alive, standing there in front of us, it was not something he or we should take for granted. God had delivered him from potentially fatal accidental electrocution, and later from an arson attack. And his emotional life, which had broken down about a year earlier through a combination of personal factors and the stresses of life in Christian mission, had been restored by God's grace. God had given him his life back. So we praised God with him: for his faithfulness, his gentleness, for the angels of mercy he sends in times of need, and above all for his word – his life-giving word.

We have already seen in chapter 7, that when the Psalmist needed an answer to the problem of sin, he knew where (and where alone) to look – to God himself.

Likewise, when he is conscious of those things that threaten his life in one way or another (see chapter 11), he knows where the only source of true life is to be found – in God. And so in all the verses where he asks for life (see the introduction to this section), it is on the foundation of something that he simultaneously affirms about God. As I analysed these 14 verses, I saw that they could be divided into two groups: those that appeal for life on the basis of the character of God, and those that appeal for life on the basis of the word of God. The source of life flows from what God is like and what God has said.

## THE CHARACTER OF GOD

### 1. God's Righteousness

> How I long for your precepts!
>   Preserve my life in your righteousness (v40).

Verse 40 may come as a surprise to some because we may be inclined to think of God's righteousness in terms of judgment, wrath and punishment – something we can never match up to and which always therefore stands over us like a measuring rod. Martin Luther tells us that he used to think that, and it puzzled him greatly, therefore, what Paul could possibly mean when he wrote that righteousness from God is *revealed in the Gospel* (Rom. 1:17). In the law, yes, how in the Gospel?

Although of course it is true that the negative judgment of God against sinners is an outworking of his righteous character, the surprising fact is that the righteousness of God is far more often associated with his salvation in the

Old Testament than with wrath and condemnation. You can check it out with a concordance if you like and look up all the occurrences of the words 'righteous' or 'righteousness' as applied to God. The LORD (*Yahweh*) is the God who vindicates, delivers, saves and rescues people. That is, he gets them out of a wrong situation and puts them right. And that's what 'doing righteousness' means. So, as Isaiah 45:21 says, he is 'a righteous God and a Saviour'. That does not mean 'a righteous God, but nevertheless in spite of that, he sometimes does some saving too.' The two phrases are synonymous. The LORD is a righteous God, and therefore he is the Saviour of his people out of their sin and slavery.

Other Psalmists frequently make this connection too. Read Psalms 35:24-28, 37:5-10 and 40:9 and then answer the following questions.

Psalm 35:24-28
- *What do you think is the background context of this appeal?*
- *What will it mean for the Psalmist if God acts on his behalf in righteousness?*
- *What will it mean for those who were attacking him?*

Psalm 37:5-10
- *This is not so much an appeal as a celebration. What words does the writer link up in poetic parallelism?*
- *Look at verse 10. Is it possible then to contrast God's love and God's righteousness and set them off one against the other? Why do we sometimes do that?*

Psalm 40:9-10
- *The Psalmist says he is going to 'preach righteousness'. What do you think he means by that?*

This is just the tip of the iceberg. In the Old Testament the righteousness of God means God in action putting things right. Putting things right will involve both identifying and punishing those who are doing wrong, and vindicating and uplifting those who are being wronged – the innocent party in a lawsuit, the oppressed in a situation of injustice. For the latter it would be like getting their life back. For somebody falsely accused of a capital offence, it would literally be having their life spared.

So now we can make sense of why our Psalmist asks God to preserve his life because of his righteousness. He is not saying, 'Save me God because I am righteous, or because I deserve your favour, or can claim your attention because I've earned your blessing.' No, he pleads, 'Save me God, but only because you are righteous. You are the God whose righteous acts of salvation and deliverance are part of our national history. Your righteousness is the Good News on which I rest my hope of life.'

We know, of course, in the light of the New Testament, that the saving righteousness of God was ultimately demonstrated on the cross. As Paul explains in Romans, the sacrifice of Christ was simultaneously God's righteous judgment on sin and his saving righteousness for sinners. That is why he can say

> I am not ashamed of the gospel, because it is the power of God for the salvation of everyone who believes: first for the Jew, then for the Gentile. For in the gospel a righteousness from God is revealed, a righteousness that is by faith from first to last, just as it is written: 'The righteous will live by faith' (Rom. 1:16-17).

It took Martin Luther some time to understand this, and in fact it was through the Psalms that he came to do so. What many people don't know about Luther is that before he became the famous reformer, he spent years as an Old Testament lecturer at Wittenberg University. And it was as he was working his way steadily through teaching the Psalms that he began to understand that 'the righteousness of God' meant his saving righteousness. From that perspective learned in the Psalms, the puzzling text in Romans came to make perfect sense and led him to his great recovery of the truth of justification by grace through faith.

### 2. God's Compassion

> Let your compassion come to me that I may live,
>    for your law is my delight (v77).

'We have given our stomachs to the Lord' is what some Africans say instead of the English expression 'give your heart to the Lord'. The stomach for them symbolizes the centre of their being. For the Hebrews, the seat of emotions was even lower down – in the bowels. That's where you really feel stuff – especially pity and sympathy. The word for compassion here is a beautiful word that speaks of that inner tender emotion that you feel deep down inside, 'in your guts' as we might say. That's where God feels his pity and compassion for us. It is the inner movement of his feelings of tender compassion towards the needy.

As we already saw in Section 3, this is a term found on God's name-badge in the Old Testament. It is of the essence of God's personal identity. It was first heard by Moses when God proclaimed his name to him, in the cleft of the rock.

> And he passed in front of Moses, proclaiming, 'The LORD, the LORD, the compassionate and gracious God, slow to anger, abounding in love and faithfulness, maintaining love

to thousands, and forgiving wickedness, rebellion and sin. Yet he does not leave the guilty unpunished' (Ex. 34:6-7).

We already saw in chapter 7 how much the compassion and grace of God meant to this Psalmist in relation to sin. Here it becomes part of his quest for life.

- *Psalm 103 also relates God's compassion to the gift of life in all its fullness. Read it through now, savouring*
- *the life-enriching blessings of verses 1-5*
- *the link with righteousness in verses 6-7*
- *the echo of Exodus 34:6 in verse 8*
- *the comparison with parental compassion in verse 13*

This is the spirituality that nourished our Psalmist also. He wants life, so he runs to the compassion of God, encouraging us to do the same.

- *The classic text about God's compassion, Exodus 34:6-8, echoes like a tolling bell through the Old Testament. Read through each of the following passages where it occurs, noting the context and background in each case, and how much the Old Testament believers relished and relied upon this bedrock truth about their God. Why did they rely upon it so much? Can you think of any New Testament passages where the same truth is expressed, in different words, in the light of the cross?*
- *Numbers 14:18*
- *Nehemiah 9:17*
- *Psalm 86:15*
- *Psalm 145:8*
- *Joel 2:13*
- *Jonah 4:2*

## 3. God's Love

> See how I love your precepts;
>   preserve my life, O LORD, according to your love (v159).

Two different Hebrew words are used here: both are translated 'love' in English and both can be used of either humans or God. *Hesed* ('your love'), means covenantally faithful love, committed loyalty to a relationship. And it is also one of the defining characteristics of Yahweh as God. So much so that Psalm 136 repeats it 26 times – in every verse – 'for his love endures for ever' (literally, 'for unto eternity is his *hesed*').

The Psalmist wants life, so he appeals to God's love, because love is life-giving. Even in ordinary human relationships we know that. When somebody loves you, life is better! People have literally been loved back to life and health. Love is what supports and revives people, lifts them out of the depths of sorrow and pain. How many great novels and movies have celebrated this fact in all its epic proportions? Committed love is the source of all that makes life worth living.

How much more true is it, then, that the love of God is life-giving? Indeed, Psalm 63:3 puts God's love above life itself.

> Because your love is better than life,
>   my lips will glorify you.

And of course, it is the essence of the gospel itself – it is the love of God that brings eternal life, for 'God so loved the world that he gave his one and only Son, that whoever believes in him shall not perish but have eternal life.'

When our Psalmist longs for God to give him life, or to renew and restore, or to preserve his life, he doesn't merely draw God's attention to the awful plight he is in. He doesn't just say 'Look at me, God.' He says, 'Lord, give me life because of who you are. You are the righteous, compassionate, loving God. That is your character. And on that basis I appeal to you to pour your own life into mine. Give me life!'

Where do you go when you know your life needs renewal and refreshment? Where do you go to get a life? Books? Conferences? A Christian holiday? Special courses or retreats? The latest spiritual technique?

Have you tried God?

But when you do, make sure it is the God of the Bible to whom you turn – not some figment of your own imagination, or somebody else's successfully marketed recipe for the good life (spiritually speaking of course). No, seek this God, the LORD God, the living God of Scripture – the God of righteousness, compassion and love.

● *Psalm 119 links the renewal of life to God's righteousness, compassion and love. What other characteristics or attributes of God could you add to that list? Try to support your answers with specific Bible passages.*

● *Review your list. If we ask God for a renewed life, what impact should it have on us, and what does that mean for you in practice when you finish this Bible study and go back to 'life in the real world'?*

## THE WORDS OF GOD

Out of the 14 verses in which the Psalmist asks God to renew his life or let him live, eight times he links the request to some dimension of the word of God with the phrase, 'according to . . .' Then he inserts three of his favourite expressions for the word of God (see the Introduction for the eight different Hebrew expressions the Psalmist uses to talk about the word of God). When the Psalmist asks God for life, he asks for it according to God's *word* (three times), God's *promise* (three times) and God's *laws* (twice). We will look at each of these in turn.

## 1. 'Your word'

Review the following three verses, identifying the main threats to life referred to.

> I am laid low in the dust;
> preserve my life according to your word (v25).

> Turn my eyes away from worthless things;
> preserve my life according to your word (v37).

> I have suffered much;
> preserve my life, O LORD, according to your word (v107).

The three verses refer to different threatening experiences, but they have a single solution – the word of God.

- *What is it about the word of God that is life-giving in such circumstances?*
- *Can you, or your group, testify to prayer like the Psalmist's being answered through the word of God in your own similar experience?*

When we speak of the word of God, we normally mean the collection of Scriptures, Old Testament and New Testament, that we call the Bible. These Old Testament believers, of course, only had some portions of that, depending on when they lived, and they loved and revered the Scriptures they had (as this Psalmist demonstrates). But they knew a thing or two about the word of God in a wider and deeper sense also.

In particular they associated it with the power of God in creation. We know this from the first chapter of the Bible, of course, where God spoke his word and stuff happened. The Psalmists revelled in it. Read Psalm 33:6-9.

> By the word of the LORD were the heavens made,
>   their starry host by the breath of his mouth.
>
> He gathers the waters of the sea into jars;
>   he puts the deep into storehouses.
>
> Let all the earth fear the LORD;
>   let all the people of the world revere him.
>
> For he spoke, and it came to be;
>   he commanded, and it stood firm.

It is easy for us to become so familiar with biblical teaching on creation that we stop being astonished at the incredible scale of what is affirmed in this beautiful poetry. All the information that is contained in our whole universe – from the equations that govern galaxies and the whole space-time continuum, down to the stupendous complexity of the information in the DNA contained in every cell of your body – was there in the word of God that brought it into existence and sustains it every day. The stars in the universe? God's breath. The oceans on the planet? God's got them in a jam jar. The whole planet earth? It's only here because God commanded it.

If, then, the word of God is the source of all life anywhere in the universe, no wonder the Psalmist figures it must be the best place to go if it's life you need. Go to the living God. Get life from his living word. As Charles Wesley wrote in his hymn, 'O for a thousand tongues': 'He speaks, and listening to his voice/New life the dead receive.'

## 2. 'Your promise'

*Read verses 50, 116 and 154 below.* They connect the Psalmist's desire for life to God's promise. In each case, notice what he wants specifically, which he believes the promises of God will supply.

> My comfort in my suffering is this:
>    Your promise preserves my life (v50).

> Sustain me according to your promise, and I will live;
>    do not let my hopes be dashed (v116).

> Defend my cause and redeem me;
>    preserve my life according to your promise (v154).

Comfort, hope and deliverance are the key words – comfort in suffering, hope to sustain him in times of weakness, rescue from vicious attack. And he looks to God's promises in such circumstances.

We are familiar with the many great and precious promises we read in the New Testament, but what were the specific promises this Old Testament believer would have known?

## 3. 'Your laws'

We can understand God giving life through his word and his promises, but would we have thought of asking God

for life 'according to your laws'? Note the word that is put
in parallel with 'your laws' in each of the verses below.

> Hear my voice in accordance with your love;
>     preserve my life, O LORD, according to your laws (v149).

> Your compassion is great, O LORD;
>     preserve my life according to your laws (v156).

The reason we may find this puzzling is because we hear
echoes, in the back of our minds, of the stern words of the
Apostle Paul in Romans and Galatians about how the law
brings condemnation and death. But it is important to see
Paul's writing in the context of the conflict he was
involved in theologically with those who had turned the
law into a burden. Punctilious keeping of the law was the
defining mark and criterion for such people of their
membership of God's covenant people, and it therefore
also functioned as an exclusion zone for all non-Jews. Paul
himself had lived that way to the utmost degree, he tells
us in Philippians 3:1-6, but now he had found
righteousness and salvation only through faith in Christ. It
was faith, not law that was the primary requirement. But
then, that was also true in the Old Testament! Paul's
quarrel was not with the Old Testament, but with those
who had distorted it into a system that had lost touch with
its true heart – relationship with God through faith in his
promise and trust in his grace.

We should remember that Psalm 119 (and the others
that celebrate God's law, like Psalm 1 and 19), is part of the
Scriptures that Paul knew and loved. He believed what
this Psalmist believed, and doubtless would and could
have prayed the prayer in the verses above.

So why then does the Psalmist ask for life 'in
accordance with your laws'? What is there in the law that

was life-giving? Well, notice again those two words that he associates with God's law – love and compassion. Where did the Israelites learn of the love and compassion of God? From their stories, yes, but also from the laws that God had given them.

● *In many of their laws, the Israelites were commanded to show love and compassion to others, and in that way to imitate God himself. Look them up and make a note of the particular way in which compassion (sometimes life-saving compassion) was commanded*

1. The refugee slave (Deut. 23:15-16)
2. The poor debtor (Deut. 15:7-11; 24:6,10-13)
3. The poor labourer (Deut. 24:14-15)
4. The landless and family-less (Deut. 14:28-29; 24:19-22)
5. The disabled (Lev. 19:14)
6. The foreigner (Ex. 23:9; Lev. 19:33-34)

Why should Israel behave like this? Because this was 'the way of the LORD'. Yahweh was the God of compassion, and so he exercised loving care for the needy. The author of Psalm 146:7-9 knew this, and he knew it from the laws, such as those above. This then was to be the model for Israelites.

> For the LORD your God is God of gods and Lord of Lords, the great God, mighty and awesome, who shows no partiality and accepts no bribes. He defends the cause of the fatherless and the widow, and loves the alien, giving him food and clothing. And you are to love those who are aliens, for you yourselves were aliens in Egypt (Deut. 10:17-19).

Indeed, God told Israel that he had given them his law to preserve and enhance their life. Obedience would be good for them and sustain long life in the land of promise. Deuteronomy makes this point repeatedly. So much so, that in appealing to the Israelites to follow God's law when they get into the land, Moses tells them that they are being faced with a choice between life and death.

> This day I call heaven and earth as witnesses against you that I have set before you life and death, blessings and curses. Now choose life, so that you and your children may live and that you may love the LORD your God, listen to his voice, and hold fast to him. For the LORD is your life, and he will give you many years in the land he swore to give to your fathers, Abraham, Isaac and Jacob (Deut. 30:19-20).

Now we can see why the Psalmist links his desire for life with God's law. He is saying, in effect, 'Lord, I want you to restore my life, and I know from your law that that is what you want too. Your law tells me that you are the God who cares for the poor, the needy and the alien. And that is what I am, what I feel like right now. So, Lord, please renew and protect my life – just as you say in your laws.'

Again and again we find that this person finds all he needs in the Scriptures. That is where he learns about God, about God's ways and character, about God's words, promises and laws. No wonder then that he appeals to God according to the Scriptures that he knows so well. It is an example we need to follow a lot more than we do. The Psalmist prays for renewal of life.

## RENEWAL AND ITS EFFECTS

Reading again through the list of 14 verses in which the Psalmist prays for renewal of life, we notice that he sometimes adds a word of 'motivation' to God to answer his prayer. Something will happen, if only God gives him his life back. Well, for the Psalmist it's fairly obvious what those things are. We've looked at them already. He will receive comfort in sorrow, hope to sustain him, strength to keep on keeping on, courage in the face of suffering and hostility. We know about these things. We can identify with the Psalmist.

But what's in it for God? What will God get if he answers this person's prayer and gives him a new lease of life, or protects his life from the danger he may be in? Look again at the first and last of the list of prayers for life. Notice the particular resolve the Psalmist makes, should the Lord allow him to live.

> Do good to your servant, and I will live;
>   I will obey your word (v17).

> Let me live that I may praise you,
>   and may your laws sustain me (v175).

Two things stand out: obedience and praise. In fact, it is worth noticing that the first time the Psalmist asks God for life, it is so that God will have his obedience; the last time he does so – in the penultimate verse of the whole psalm – it is so that God will have all his praise. There is something very healthy about this. It stands out against any self-centred bargaining that is at the core of 'prosperity teaching'.

*Obedience*. Why should God be good to me and let me live? So that I can get on with doing what he wants to be done. Why should any of us, sinners that we are, be spared to enjoy life at all, except to find our fulfilment of life in loving, serving and obeying our Maker and Redeemer? There is a wonderful dynamic cycle of life within Old Testament faith, which you find running through the law and the psalms especially. God's blessing gives us life. As we live, we obey him in response to his grace and gift of blessing. That in turn leads to further blessing, which leads to renewed obedience. It all flows from grace, through gratitude, into obedience, back to blessing and onwards to God's own glory and pleasure.

*Praise*. Towards the end of this psalm in which we have found so much lament, struggle, suffering and exhaustion, is a longing for life – so that God can be praised.

There is a touching pre-resurrection faith at work here. Old Testament believers did not lack a growing awareness that God had power over death and that their relationship with God would not be destroyed by death. But it was life here and now on God's good earth that filled most of their horizon. So the Psalmist is saying to God, 'Lord, if I die, who is going to be praising you then? My bones? The dust? Not much, I think, so let me live that I may praise you, while I have life and breath!' The same perspective comes in the similar plea for life in Psalm 30:9.

> What gain is there in my destruction,
>   in my going down into the pit?
> Will the dust praise you?
>   Will it proclaim your faithfulness?

Although the final note of the psalm is one of praise, the final verse of the psalm shows that it does not mean happy-clappy joyfulness. This person still feels like a lost sheep, in need of being found again and brought back by and to God.

It is good to remind ourselves again at this point that praise in the Bible is more than joyfulness – indeed it can function in the apparent absence of joy. It is not something we do when we have no troubles, or as a way of escaping from our troubles; we do it in the midst of them. One of the things I get annoyed about in some worship times is when the leader invites us all to 'Leave all the things that have been on our minds and bothering us before we came to church. Leave them behind and let's just come into God's presence and praise the Lord.' But what does that achieve? All it means is that you think you've been praising God, and then you go back to your troubles. They are waiting for you at the door of the church; you pick them up as you go out, but you haven't brought them into the presence of God. The Psalmists don't do that. They bring everything before God, and sometimes they throw them down in front of him and challenge him to do something and ask how long they have to wait. And that too is praise. For it is acknowledging the reality and the presence and power of God and bringing *all of life* before him.

So this Psalmist is not saying, 'Lord, restore my life and we'll all live happily ever after.' Life is not a fairy story. No, he says, 'Lord, restore my life and I will praise you with my whole being, even when I feel like a lost sheep, even when life is tough, even when I wonder where you are and when you will act.'

*Renewal* is an over-used word today that sometimes gets twisted away from its biblical roots and meaning. In some circles it seems to be a kind of spiritual narcissism. 'Look how blessed and renewed I got!'; 'You too can have the renewal we've been having, if you just do what we do.' People want renewal and blessing, but they are not perhaps so willing to live lives of obedience and praise, even in the midst of their struggle – as this Psalmist did. Yet surely, claimed renewal without obedience is a fake. And claimed renewal without sincere praise to God in the whole of life is nothing but self-focused idolatry.

**FURTHER STUDY**
Turn to Isaiah 40:28-31. We are told that if we 'hope in the Lord' our strength will be renewed. What does it mean to hope in the Lord? How should this affect the way we view struggles and difficulties?

**REFLECTION AND RESPONSE**
Make a list for yourself, or as a group, of promises from the Old Testament that bring comfort, hope and protection from God into your life.

Here are a few to get you started:

Joshua 1:5

Isaiah 43:1-2

Psalm 23

Jeremiah 29:11

Daniel 3:16-18

Add more, and claim their life-giving power for your particular needs.

# Conclusion

We have walked a long way in the company of the person who composed this marvellous psalm.

- *We have been impressed with his core commitment to the word of God and its eternal, moral truth, and challenged by the strength and passion of such a worldview.*
- *We have witnessed his longing to be guided by God and walk in God's way, finding light and learning through God's word.*
- *We have identified with his acute awareness of sin and all the horrendous damage it does in human life, and share his longing to avoid it and find in God our only answer through his forgiving grace.*
- *We have exposed some of the struggles that he was going through, externally and internally, and heard the minor keys of his laments and protests – recognizing that these are words that not only speak to us (as God's word), but also often speak for us.*
- *And we have heard his recurrent longing for life itself – the renewed, restored, abundant life, that only God can give – because of the God that he is and the things he has said.*

It would be good to finish by reading the final section of this great poem slowly and aloud. For it is here that so many of the psalm's themes surface again.

> May my cry come before you, O LORD;
>    give me understanding according to your word.
> May my supplication come before you;
>    deliver me according to your promise.
> May my lips overflow with praise,
>    for you teach me your decrees.

May my tongue sing of your word,
　for all your commands are righteous.
May your hand be ready to help me,
　for I have chosen your precepts.
I long for your salvation, O LORD,
　and your law is my delight.
Let me live that I may praise you,
　and may your laws sustain me.
I have strayed like a lost sheep.
　Seek your servant,
　for I have not forgotten your commands (vv169-176).

And as we reflect on his final prayer in the last verse, isn't it a great comfort to know that at the end of the day, as at the end of this psalm, it is the responsibility of the shepherd to find the lost sheep, not the responsibility of the sheep to find the shepherd?

May the Lord himself seek and find each one of us, as we seek him, his word and his will for our lives.

# ENDNOTES

[1] At least, so far as I am aware, though on one occasion after making this point I had a mother bring me a very colourful drawing by her indignant child of a tooth fairy, wings and all, to challenge my rash dismissal. If I were to revise the above statement to: 'In the world of children's literature and imagination, tooth fairies have wings', I would be making a true statement, because children, and books written for them, are all objective realities in themselves.

[2] This in itself should raise some suspicions when we think of what happened in the lives of many in the Bible whose lives, when God got involved in them, were to all intents and purposes turned upside down or virtually wrecked.

[3] While this prayer may occur in various grammatical forms the word 'understand' or 'understanding' remains in common.

[4] The term is borrowed from the book by Alan Mann, *Atonement for a 'Sinless' Society* (Milton Keynes: Paternoster, 2005). Mann's point, of course, is not that postmodern western society is actually sinless in the sense of not doing wrong, but that it has lost any sense of the meaning of sin. It has become a culture that lacks a conceptual box into which the biblical understanding of sin can fit. His book offers some penetrating, challenging and at times controversial discussion of how the biblical gospel can relate to such a culture.

[5] Genesis 3-11 shows this graphically, as does Paul's commentary on it in Romans 1 and 2.

[6] 1 Peter 3:13-17 is particularly helpful in this respect.

[7] For further reading see Andrew Perriman (ed.), *Faith, Health and Prosperity* (Carlisle: Paternoster, 2003).

Keswick Ministries was set up in response to demand to take the excellent Bible teaching of the three week summertime Lake District Keswick Convention and make it available throughout the year and around the world. Its work is aimed at Christians of all backgrounds who have a desire to learn from God's Word and let it change their lives.

Keswick Ministries is committed to achieving its aims by:

- providing Bible based training courses for church leaders, youth workers and young people, preachers and teachers, and all those who want to develop their skills and learn more

- promoting the use of books, tapes, videos and CDs so that Keswick's teaching ministry is brought to a wider audience at home and abroad

- producing TV and radio programmes so that superb Bible talks can be broadcast to you at home

- publishing up-to-date details of Keswick's exciting news and events on our website so that you can access material and purchase Keswick products on-line

- publicising Bible teaching events in the UK and overseas so that Christians of all ages are encouraged to attend 'Keswick' meetings closer to home and grow in their faith

- putting the residential accommodation of the Convention Centre at the disposal of churches, youth groups, Christian organisations and many others, at very reasonable rates, for holidays and outdoor activities in a stunning location

If you'd like more details please look at our website (www.keswickministries.org) or contact the General Director by post, email or telephone as given below.

Keswick Ministries, PO Box 6, Keswick, Cumbria, CA12 4GJ
Tel: 017687 80075
Fax 017687 75276
Email: centre@keswickconv.com